D1577853

Financial Literacy

*Timeless concepts to turn
financial chaos into clarity*

by
Duke Kunkler

Printed in the United States of America

ISBN: 978-1-4675-2009-6

This publication was written to provide authoritative information and should be used as a general guide. It is sold with the understanding that the author is not providing legal, accounting, financial, or other licensed-professional advice. The author and publisher are not liable or responsible for any loss or damages caused directly or indirectly from the usage of the material in this publication. The stories featured in this publication are based on real people. However, the names and some personal information have been changed to protect their privacy.

Financial Literacy

*Timeless concepts to turn
financial chaos into clarity*

by
Duke Kunkler

Acknowledgement

This book is only possible because I was able to remember and utilize what my father taught me about money. Managing money was one of the dozens of subjects that he taught me. I listened as he advised others on money matters and how *all* decisions also have a financial impact. While supporting a family with four children (whom he put through college and graduate school), I learned as he started from nothing and slowly increased his income and net worth to put him in the top 1%.

Table of Contents

Preface

My interest in investing and money matters, in addition to a father who is an accountant, has attracted people with personal-finance questions since my teens. In high school I was doing tax returns for other people and had invested most of my lifetime earnings in individual stocks and a bar of silver. As an adult, it has been frustrating that there is still no single resource that I can point to for those looking for all of the basic concepts that everyone so desperately needs to build a solid financial foundation. There are many sources for financial opinions, but where do you learn how to *think* about money concepts? Yes, there are bestselling books by financial-planners and blogs with zillions of insightful remarks to consider. But despite these resources, others still contact me for assistance after they have read these books, used financial software, and, many times, *already* have employed financial advisors. Professional experts ask me for assistance with their own dilemmas in personal finance and investing; experts such as pension managers, hedge fund traders, accountants, tax attorneys, venture capitalists, 401(k) administrators, stock brokers, money managers, and finance PhDs. Even these experienced professionals are rarely grounded in all of the basics in how to think about money. Sadly, many people are certain that they are living below their means until glaring deficiencies are meticulously mapped out for them. This book was written to highlight how you should be thinking about your finances as you evaluate life-defining decisions for yourself. Following the advice in this book will provide you the essential financial foundation and prepare you to move toward advanced topics.

This book is divided into two sections. The first section is about concepts, both financial concepts and investing concepts. The second section is step-by-step instructions on how to invest in the stock market and then how to comprehensively manage your money.

Preface

Introduction

The Financial Predicament

Many financial decisions are a part of life in which people have the least amount of confidence. There is only one methodology to bolster your confidence and neutralize the noise and nonsense surrounding financial matters. To illustrate this methodology, first, let me ask you two financial questions:

• Is $400 a month an affordable car payment?
• Is 4% an acceptable return for an investment?

The correct answer to both of these is: you have not been given enough information to reach any kind of conclusion. This sample highlights that you cannot form any financial answer until you have enough reference points to reach some threshold of an informed opinion. Those of you who had an opinion about those two questions did so only because you already have some reference points from which to draw. Most people make critical financial decisions with no idea about how to make those decisions. This example illustrates that every financial number is a useless data point—a meaningless numerical symbol that is floating in a void. It is only through building reference points around a number that you can discover its meaning and relevance. Only when you have these reference points can you apply financial principles and arrive at a proficient evaluation for your particular situation.

The more financial reference points you have, the more accurate and precise your decision-making will become within the fuzzy subject of finance. For example, when someone says that your retirement plan needs to take into account a 3% inflation rate, I can reference where they found that number and what it does and does not represent. When someone else says that you should plan for 6.3% inflation in your retirement I also know how this number was calculated plus what it does and does not represent. Whom would you trust the most to help you—the 3% person, the 6.3% person, or someone who knows many inflation calculations and statistics? Wait until you start looking at the staggering number of conflicting stock market returns. Many financial advisors like to distill things down to make them simple with an optimistic bias toward their solutions so that their clients can understand and buy their products. Whether an issue is simple or complex, favorable or unfavorable, you need unfiltered accurate facts and full historical information to make the best decisions that will have any financial impact on your life.

Managing money with a lack of financial principles leaves many people unsure if they are making the best financial decisions. One by one, the concepts that will be covered will illuminate the financial labyrinth that you have already been operating in, albeit unknowingly. The sooner you are aware of these concepts, the sooner you can course-correct toward financial targets that are important to you. Since this book is for a broad audience, individual readers may find that some advice appears too simple or too complicated, too far below or above their current financial circumstances. The ideas included in this book are those that, in my experience, are needed the most; even by people who have significant incomes, assets, and advisors.

The 10 Financial Dilemmas

Money management is often only equated with budgeting or financial transactions, but to me, it describes all that you do that has a financial effect. For many, managing your personal finances is often a nebulous, mysterious subject. In my view there are 10 inherent reasons why this will always be so. Let's go through them so you have an idea about what you are up against and why the information in this book is so important:

1. Money has no innate structure:

The order and purpose for a handful of cash can only come from the mind of its owner. Cash does not come with an instruction manual; it is simply an inert transferable store of value. In the absence of conceptual order from the mind of its owner, money dissipates through predictable and foreseeable paths of behavior. Managing your money is just a value puzzle—without rules—that you play alone. To illustrate this, if you had $100 in your hand, do you:

- Spend it on food or car insurance?
- Donate it to a charity or add it to your retirement account?
- Buy new shoes because a store has a 20% off sale for today only?
- Buy a stock option in the latest hot company?
- Set it aside to save for an expensive home repair or jewelry gift?

How do you decide whether you can afford to buy anything with it? Is there any difference between the options presented in these questions?

By the end of this book you will easily answer all of these questions for yourself, in as much precision as you desire; and you will have a framework to assist you in all of your financial decisions.

Money and value can be physical objects, but every decision you make about what to do with them is entirely conceptual. How you handle $100 in cash or property may appear trivial, but underlying your choice are real financial concepts—such as assignment, allocation, opportunity costs, and the imminent increase or decrease of your current net worth and monetary future. You are already applying these concepts to every single financial decision that you make, either knowingly or unknowingly. For example, most people have no idea that they must separate any physical amount of money they have from the financial concepts that will guide where it is to be employed. Financial concepts must be the starting point in all money management. What you physically do with your money is only the execution that will produce the financial targets you have in mind.

There can be a significant financial difference between what you believe you are doing with your money and property, and the measurable financial reality of your behavior according to financial principles. If you do not manage your money using the financial concepts of accumulation then your actions will most likely be following diffuse paths of financial dissipation.

In the simplest sense, if there is $100 in your pocket, you are the only barrier between keeping that $100, multiplying it, or being broke. More simply, the financial concepts you know and choose to employ upon that physical $100 will determine your financial present and future. If you do not operate your life with any financial concepts (or, worse, with incorrect concepts), then your financial decisions will likely be leaving you much poorer than you should be.

When you have no guiding concepts for money, then there is only one item on your mind: that physical $100 in your hand. When this happens, our brains automatically think about ways to spend it and then we buy things until it is all gone. You've already heard the cliché that describes this: "Money burns a hole in their pocket." In the absence of financial concepts, most people follow these paths of financial trouble: poor career management, spending more than their income, incurring personal debts, investing poorly, letting the value of their assets unnecessarily fall, paying too much in taxes, no emergency fund for unexpected events, letting inflation erode their financial capability, and allowing exposure to unaffordable risks that could have been reasonably insured.

There are seemingly invisible financial opportunities and expenses that are amassing around you. If you fail to manage your finances with awareness of these, there will be an ever-growing gap between your current financial reality and how much more prosperous it could have been. This gap is created by the difference between financial awareness and ignorance; between the financial optimum you could have built knowing financial principles and your current financial state. One of the goals of this book is to help you minimize any gaps from your own optimum level of wealth and get on track to meet your own financial goals. If you are not using the basic financial concepts that will be presented, money in your hands will have far more difficulty in supporting a sustainable lifestyle for yourself in the future.

So how do you go about deciding among the vast number of choices that you have available for that $100? Then the next $100 that comes along? No wonder so many people avoid the subject or are never sure about what to do. Some people only have a vague idea about their spending while others meticulously use budgeting software unaware that it cannot address most financial issues. You will need to direct a wide range of financial decisions throughout your life and you will need some basis to make these decisions for your financial benefit. Many people do not realize that they are playing the financial "game of life" poorly until they notice that their peers-in-income are talking about large purchases or early retirement that they themselves could never afford. Anything that $100 can buy is simultaneously a legitimate use of money or a costly financial misstep; the difference depends on which financial concepts you are employing for that money. Financial concepts you personally employ will change with your level of knowledge, circumstances, and capability.

2. Most financial viewpoints are contradictory:

Performing a particular activity can be an expense to one person and yet income to another. A great investment for one person can be a grievous investment error to another. Extremely different advice can be appropriate for people with different capabilities. There are no financial platitudes that always apply to everyone because every single financial move is a double-edged sword of commitment vs. opportunity costs. Some find these financial contradictions uncomfortable so they contract and stick with a simple tactic to the exclusion of others that could have significantly improved their financial status. When you read or hear contradictory advice, how do you know which one to follow? Some of the viewpoints that you should consider are: Which advice has helped the most people? Which is the most relevant to my capability and circumstances? Which ones have a higher probability of occurring? What is the likelihood of their maximum loss or maximum gain? It is by having the most financial perspectives at your disposal that your financial decisions will be the most robust for whatever may happen in the future. A friend once asked my father, an experienced estate executor, to review his Will that was drafted by an attorney. Within three minutes, my father detailed how the most likely scenarios to play out in the future and would have resulted in the exact *opposite* of the wishes of my friend. So the friend had a new Will drawn up to avoid those problems. The more reference points, viewpoints, and scenarios that are considered, the more accurate and successful your financial decision-making will become.

3. Many financial decisions depend upon a guess about the future:

Unfortunately, many financial decisions that must be made today are based on fuzzy predictions about the future. For example, how many months until your house sells, what will your tax-bracket be in 20 years, how much extra money could you save in 7 years, are interest rates lower than average or higher than average, how long until you find another job, etc. While you cannot predict the future, the more effort you put into a financially important decision, the more likely you will make the most durable choice. Over time, you will develop your skill at likely scenarios and be better prepared to know when and how to react as circumstances play out, instead of getting financially blind-sided by predictable events.

4. Knowing everything about money is impossible and keeping up-to-date with financial news is an endless treadmill:

There is a subjective line between knowing enough to competently address a financial issue (or managing a professional performing this service for you) and getting on a never-ending treadmill to learn more about the ever-changing details. The extreme version of this treadmill is "analysis paralysis," where instead of deciding on an issue after you have more than enough information, you continually choose to wait for more information. Once you get beyond the basics, there are two types of financial decisions that can become a never-ending treadmill. First, there is trying to learn everything currently available today (i.e. the cheapest car insurance, which bank has the highest paying savings account, what are the rules for this type of tax deduction for next year?). Then there is trying to become knowledgeable enough to forecast the future (will this stock be higher in 10 years, which currency will gain in strength over the next 3 years, which fixed-income mutual fund will not drop in value over the next two years?). There is a line between where to use your time and where to use the expertise of others. For example, after you have several insurance quotes for your particular situation, is it worth spending several days of full-time effort to save a small amount on that bill? Any value that you might receive must be compared to the time, effort, and cost that you'll invest to receive that value. In many cases a little effort is all that is necessary. When large numbers are at stake for you (re-allocating your retirement savings near retirement age, buying a home, making a large single investment), then you either need to be closer to having professional knowledge yourself or to hire someone with that professional knowledge. For better or worse, you are solely responsible and accountable for all of your financial decisions. To carry out this task requires an ongoing routine of some minimum level of financial learning and observing to figure out where your subjective line is for doing something personally or finding and managing experts on your behalf.

5. Financial decisions are not confidence builders:

The elements of financial decisions are simple, but you may never be 100% certain about a financial decision. All you can do is confirm that you used sound financial judgment for an event but not the actual outcome of a single event itself. When you are looking back in hindsight, it will seem that there was a better way to go about achieving a financial goal, to handle a tough situation, or to get a better investment return. It is common to only focus on missed opportunities or a lucky gain; you need to build some psychological grit so you do not retreat from future financial decisions just because you were stung once.

I remember talking to someone about a financial decision they were facing. He had a month to decide whether to keep putting money into an asset that he was trying to sell. It was easy to make some calculations and find the break-even date when he should walk-away from the asset. But we ended up having a few conversations and going over scenarios and probabilities and from this effort a patient decision was made that happened to unfold favorably. This decision hinged on an unknowable factor over which he had no control. There is an old saying, "Every crystal ball is cloudy." Many financial decisions must be made under similarly cloudy conditions. A vague sense of "likelihood" is the most control that you can hope for in financial decisions about the uncertain future.

There is no calculator or person who can say "you made the absolute correct choice." It is the nature of financial decisions that you cannot know if any decision were optimal. Afterward, you might discover that you decided poorly but got lucky, or decided wisely and had poor luck. The psychological key to making financial decisions is to get comfortable operating with a subject matter that is always fluctuating: the numbers change, the rules change, the probabilities change, and the meanings change. Another aspect of this is not to allow a few bad financial outcomes to ruin your confidence in handling normal risks. Like a champion athlete, chess player, or salesperson, you accept some failures and setbacks as part of the normal process of successfully moving forward.

6. It is common to rationalize our way out of financial restraints:

Governments, companies, and individuals are forever finding new ways to justify spending beyond their means. Sadly, there is an ongoing struggle over where, when, and how to set spending priorities for our limited budgets. Some people are natural tight-wads while others cannot save a dime even with a lottery windfall. Most people quickly spend all the money they receive each month. It can be frustrating to learn the lesson "work first, play later;" and it can be similarly difficult to learn "save first, spend later." The psychological discipline to save some of the money that you receive determines whether your future will be moving toward a financial victory or calamity. Saving money does not have to translate into a vow of poverty; it simply means that there must be the existence of some restraint; some frugality. Whether you are in charge of a country, a non-profit institution, a company, or a household, all costs must be constrained below the income or eventually there must be some type of very painful insolvency and liquidation. It takes zero skill to spend money but it does take discipline to manage it prudently. You are the only one who can give yourself part of your paycheck; and if you are paying it all to others each month, you are literally working for their financial benefit and not your own. The finances of a government or business are identical to the finances of a household: you can be the manager of a solvent institution by using restraint, or you will be in need of a charitable bailout.

Hopefully, you may become more motivated to save when presented with the reality that will be outlined later. There are always a few proud cheapskates who recoil from spending, and many minor savers. But unfortunately, most people need to experience either a financial disaster or slowly reach a financial breaking point before they reluctantly consider adopting a serious routine of regular saving.

7. Financial decisions test your psychological weaknesses:

A lack of money can heighten your desperation; extra money in your wallet can exaggerate your greed, guilt, or entitlement; putting your money into investments with risk will exaggerate your fears. These powerful emotions blind us to reality, force us to make decisions contrary to our best interest, and at worst, entice us to act without integrity. The more aware you are of financial principles and guidelines, the less likely you will fall prey to emotional decisions with poor results, instead of logical decisions that will preserve and add to your financial stability. The smartest financial choices can be the most difficult to make psychologically, while many of the easy choices leave us poorer than we should have been. Emotions around money can run very high even with a sound financial plan; without a plan, it is likely that poor decisions will be compounded and exacerbated by your emotions.

Few people reveal exactly how they manage their money, even with their partner. What people do with their money is rarely talked about in most societies so what the average person is doing remains a mystery. Aside from a few general studies, it is difficult to learn exactly what others are doing that may be better than how you are handling your own money. Many spouses or partners also keep secret accounts and credit cards for spending privacy. Since you don't clearly know what others are doing with their money, it is an area of life that makes people uncertain about their own finances.

8. Every financial decision is a permanent tradeoff among constraints:

Each financial decision you make with financial consequences has a permanent effect; there is only the forward movement of time. Each decision is a choice among mutually-exclusive options for buy, sell, wait, hold, spend, save, and invest. No matter what your resources, your spending is constrained by the amount of cash and credit you currently have available. You cannot spend the same money twice; you can only spend within 100% of your financial resources at any given point in time. Other tradeoffs include where you place your money, such as safe or risky, liquid or illiquid, taxable or non-taxable, or exposed to the fluctuations of interest rates, equities, or currencies. No matter what the spending or investment choice, you are making decisions that cannot be avoided or later reversed.

9. Trends last for long periods and then change when they are least expected:

There are market trends that can last for very long periods of time. This activity lulls people into thinking things will always be this way over years or decades and then the markets or politicians will abruptly reverse course catching most everyone off-guard. Some examples: commodities, currencies, interest rates, industry groups, technologies, real estate, stock values, and gold. When most people are convinced that a trend will continue is when the risk is increasing for events that will start a new trend in the opposite direction. Normally, few people are prepared for any market reversal and they alone protect themselves or profit while most people suffer financial losses.

10. Money affects every area of your life:

The amount of money flowing through your hands determines your options for health treatment, education, vacation, legal advice, and influences who your friends and associates may be. Your past decisions, current desires, and future plans are all financially linked. If you overstep financially in one area, it will eventually affect many other unrelated areas. To effectively move toward all of your dreams, you cannot step blindly. Yet many rewarding parts of life are made by taking a leap without a net. A few examples of the unknown are: moving to a new city or country, taking on a large project, changing careers, creating something new, starting a business, or running for a political office. You do not know how they will end or what the total cost will be before you start. However, these decisions must still be made and their financial effects will impact all that you do.

These 10 inherent problems all conspire to generate mystery and difficulty around financial knowledge and decisions. Whether you want to be or not, you are figuratively a player on the field of the money game of life. Unless you learn the rules of this money game, you may find yourself unknowingly losing to the experienced and knowledgeable players. Plus, you need to learn what to do in order to grab some financial victories for yourself. So let's get started on the concepts, tools, and practices to address these and get your financial life on its maximum trajectory.

FINANCIAL CONCEPTS

Offering readers a few particular rules may help some people manage their money. But this does not convey any of the financial reasoning or supportive arguments so that you'll know how to modify money rules to your particular situation. It is my view that understanding how to *think* about money is far more important than applying a rote rule. It is so important that the conceptual sections of this book are larger than the sections laying out the explicit rules. Once you really understand financial reasoning, you will be able to develop, refine, and enhance your own approaches and rules to managing your money as well.

Winning Concept #1

The first step toward bringing clarity to your financial life is to measure and monitor all of the income, expenses, assets, and debts that you control.

You cannot hit distant financial targets or avoid foreseeable financial landmines without the insights that are available from tracking the movement of money and property flowing in and out of your control. It is mandatory for you to have some type of mechanism to track your current financial state. Do you itemize your income, expenses, account balances, and financial targets along with calibrating how well you are working toward these targets? You cannot determine that critical decision-making number that you use every day—affordability—without a thorough attempt at this process. Today, exactly how do you determine what you can afford to spend in any area of your life? Measuring and tracking your financial life is the only way to create the financial feedback from your current behavior to determine exactly where you need to make behavioral changes to reach any financial goal. This information also highlights where to shift around what you own and what you owe based on their changing values and rates. Measuring your financial life creates the financial map to determine where you are and what you need to do to reach your financial goals. Without this map you are needlessly guessing in a financial fog with potentially expensive and painful consequences.

Since financial clarity helps you to make appropriate decisions, it is natural that some businesses attempt to make that difficult by turning your money into various abstractions. For example: casinos turn your cash into chips, many businesses use points and loyalty programs, anything that is a distraction to move your focus away from money going from your wallet to theirs. People that shop with credit cards (another money abstraction) are more willing to make purchases and spend a little more than those shoppers who are holding cash. Other industries make transactions more complicated—giving you a big benefit on one part hoping that you do not notice other parts getting more expensive. For example, offering a cheap printer that is only compatible with expensive ink cartridges or a mortgage that lowers your payment but dramatically increases the length of the mortgage. Any awareness or tools that provide you more financial clarity will help you through the labyrinth of financial decisions you will be making.

Everyone I know who successfully retired in comfort by age 60 had it thoroughly mapped out to make it happen. Years ago, I read that just like every public company, rich people fill out a financial balance sheet at least once a year to assess their financial progress. Curious about what other people might be doing, I started to ask many people if they have ever filled out a personal financial balance sheet for themselves. My results confirmed what I had read: all of the financially ambitious people whom I knew had a recent balance sheet at their desk while everyone else had no idea what I was talking about.

The most important outcome from tracking your money is that you have a basis to start separating the actual money that moves through your hands from your financial concepts about how to handle that money. It is only when you develop some concepts about allocating and assigning money that you can accurately assess where your next $100 fits in. Your decisions with financial effects must first be aligned with financial concepts in order to determine where, when, and what you can afford to spend your money on.

Everyone incurs a lifetime of expenses supported by income and much of it is fairly easy to predict as one large expense. If you do not have the details of this roughly-figured out and budgeted, sooner or later your life will be under-funded and unsupported.

Tracking and monitoring your financial matters is the only diagnostic tool to determine where problems are coming from and where there are opportunities to make financial progress. It is your early alert system to highlight problems and also provides you a green light to proceed with opportunities. Very few people want to track every dollar that moves, however this may be a temporary necessity when there is a financial problem, mystery, or crisis.

As you begin monitoring your finances, here are some of the stages of financial awareness that you need to move through:

1. Knowing all of your regular cash inflows

and outflows, along with any erratic bill or income that arrives during the year.

2. Regular monitoring of ratios, values, and investment returns to make adjustments to your behavior, assets, and debts to reach financial goals.

3. Continual self-education and using professionals to proactively optimize your income, expenses, budgets, assets, debts, savings, investments, projections, taxes, legal entity structures, insurance, residence location, estate planning, and asset protection.

Managing your money requires financial data that can only come from tracking and categorizing your financial life in ways that are in alignment with financial principles. Most people operate with only two categorizations of money: spendable after-tax money and qualified money in retirement accounts with IRS rules for withdrawal. Many people believe that if they contribute some money to an IRA or 401(k) that this is all the financial planning they need to perform and the rest will take care of itself. Until you map out your financial life, you have no way of knowing if this is correct. Wouldn't you prefer to know where you are heading now so that you can do something to avoid foreseeable problems?

Moving forward financially may include decisions on every front, including a career change, moving to a different state with more opportunity, surviving the start-up losses of a new business, etc.—and every one of these decisions rests upon the details of tracking your financial life.

Winning Concept #2

Your behavior must continually improve your financial stability.

Financial stability is defined as the mandatory combination of these three actions each and every time that you receive income from any source:

1. Spending less than this income.
2. Add some of this money into a separate savings account as a reserve for expected future spending and maintenance.
3. Add some of this money into a separate investment account to purchase productive investments to be held forever. (Productive investments are defined as investments that produce income from either scheduled dividend or interest payments.)

You can do many things with new income. But these three actions build the most solid foundation for everything else that you can possibly do with your money. These steps for financial stability force you to increase your net worth and investment income every time you receive income. The basis of this concept is: your income is either permanently wasted by spending all of it or permanently preserved by saving all of it. Either throw it away on stuff or make it your investment employee forever. The easy way to create financial stability is to take part of your income and both save some and invest some; then improve your ability at both. These actions continually add to your wealth. You will start increasing your likelihood of financial success when you consider this question before you make any purchase, "Will this purchase violate my financial stability this pay period?"

This concept also highlights that there are only three things you can do with your income: spend it, save it, or invest it. To advance financially you must put money into each of these three every time you receive money from any source. If any of the elements of financial stability are missing then your current financial position will be continually falling away from its optimum. Many people with a high or increasing salary can temporarily afford many financial mistakes, but a single large financial mistake or a change in your career trajectory will quickly reveal a weak financial foundation. Regardless of your level of income, continually missing any of the three elements creates predictable financial difficulties. Families with an average or below-average income have less room to maneuver out of financial mistakes or recover from unexpected expenses. Although it never feels like it at the time, a lot of spending is purely emotional and can easily consume far more than your income. The elements of financial stability provide a simple guideline for your spending and can help minimize the missteps that result in unnecessary borrowing, a lower credit rating, or being forced to liquidate assets quickly at low prices and high tax consequences.

Winning Concept #2 is the mechanism that enables the transition from being financially helpless to financially powerful in your life. You must execute this step no matter how poor or broke you feel—otherwise you cannot improve your financial situation. Specifically, building reserves of savings is the mechanism to prevent you from borrowing money for expected purchases and unexpected expenses. Building investments is the mechanism to start earning income from your money to escape having to earn money solely from a job for the rest of your life. Yes, social security or state welfare may keep you from starving but a season does not pass without news stories of a price rise of some sort that is creating hardship for people with a low income or fixed-income retirees. Following the elements of financial stability provides you with ever-more economic control and choices on how to move through your life instead of being at the short-term whims of the global economy, politicians, or your personal career opportunities without any financial buffer. There are inevitable increases in prices and expenses for your family and your retirement, and the three elements of financial stability are the most certain way to keep ahead of them.

Financial stability also creates the capability for you to benefit when opportunities arise. I know someone who made an offer to buy an old rusty car that had been sitting in the same spot for years. This car was next to a busy road where commuters passed it by every day. My acquaintance knew very little about cars but was curious and capable, so she made a few phone calls and discovered that it would be worth a lot of money if it were rebuilt. She negotiated with the owner and bought the rusty car for $5,000. She then paid an expert to rebuild the car for $15,000 and the finished car appraised for $70,000 (with the possibility that it could increase even more in value as a collectible vehicle.) She would not have been able to do this without financial stability, plus some ambition, which allowed her to turn $20,000 into $70,000 off of an opportunity that was available to each person who drove by the car for years. In another example, the day after the stock market had a sharp drop, I knew two people who made low bids on real estate in Manhattan and Las Vegas well below the current market price. These low offers were immediately accepted from sellers unsure if they would get another offer anytime soon. Would you have had the financial stability and have been psychologically ready to make such a move during a period of financial uncertainty?

Another important aspect of financial stability is to evaluate whether your financial decisions are increasing your net worth over time. You will start, launch, and maximize your net worth from routine financial decisions that you make each month. Your net worth is your ultimate safety reserve: the more equity that you have in your home, car, investments, or anything else, the more financial options and flexibility you will have when confronted with the unpredictable drama of life.

In my teens, I decided to divide any income I received into categories for financial stability—no matter what. The next money that I received was $10 that I dutifully placed into 3 different envelopes. It felt ridiculous to split up such a tiny amount, but I knew it was the correct habit to start. I called the first envelope "The Vault" because money goes in and never comes out; this was for investments. The second envelope was labeled "Savings" for planned expenses, and the third envelope was called "Fun Money" for entertainment. Since then, having seen how the habit of dividing up all income consistently funds goals for people, it is disappointing when I hear about others who fail to do this.

Maximum financial stability is having predictable

investment income that is greater than all of your expenses for the same time period. This is the financial freedom that so many people are seeking but unsure of how to start building. If you had this amount of money, what would you be doing to manage it all? How much time, effort, resources, and procedures do you think that you would need? On a small scale, this is what you have to start doing today in order to expand into managing your ever-increasing financial resources. Time and effort to manage your financial matters must be expended. You can start with 5 minutes a month with paper and pencil, but if you want to increase your financial capacity, you may eventually need regular meetings with advisors, using software or systems to track cash flows, investments, taxes, and projects; and ever more refinement of your financial decision-making to achieve or increase your financial targets. Diligence at your own financial stability will start another transition from the problem of not having nearly enough money to an easier problem of how to best re-deploy new money coming in from new savings, dividends, interest, and investment sales. Success in any area is a reflection of your capability and discipline, and money matters are no different.

"I had to buy it—it was on sale! I saved money!"

The idea of buying items on sale or getting a discount makes people more gratified about their purchase. But using this as a tactic to actually save money is a topic that few people fully evaluate. Many people, myself included, love to mention how much I saved (and how savvy I am by implication) by doing something myself or getting a deal on a purchase. But the bulk of these "saving money" stories are just a cover story to hide an imprudent outflow of money. It does not matter how much an item is discounted if the expense is unaffordable for your level of income. You won't be the first to "save" your way into insolvency.

Let's examine this simple scenario: if you ate at a restaurant with a 10%-off coupon, did you actually save any money? This appears to be a simple question and the obvious answer is "Yes, I saved 10%." My response is that we have to hunt down that 10% savings to audit where it actually ended up and verify if any money were actually "saved" and increased your financial stability:

1. Was there an outflow of money? If yes, then there is no savings yet, the only activity that has occurred is that money has left your wallet and gone into someone else's wallet; you are left poorer. Maybe you received something of value in return, but its value is not as certain as the money that you have given up.

2. Is the cash that you saved still in a location that you regularly use for spending? If it is, then you still have not saved the 10% yet; it is more likely that you have only temporarily delayed spending that extra 10%. Instead of spending 100% on that meal, you only spent 90% and then diverted the extra 10% into another spending category—so all of the money that you would have spent without the coupon is still all gone from your wallet. This does not sound like savings yet; you have only shuffled spending from one category to another. While the coupon allowed you to consume a little more in that other category; your "saving money" activity has not added to any of the three criteria for financial stability.

3. If you did not have a coupon for this meal, would you have eaten a meal that was more than 10% cheaper either at home or some other restaurant? If yes, then you actually paid a premium for your meal under the guise of getting a discount— you have just done the opposite of saving money, you paid extra for this meal and are even poorer than you would have been without the coupon.

4. If a coupon/discount/sale is regularly offered, then there is no alleged lower price—the discounted price that you paid *is* the real price; the regular retail price is an inflated price that few people actually pay. Just because someone claims there is a discount does not make it true.

5. If you bought something cheaper than normal, was it something that you planned to resell at the normal market price for a profit? If you have not resold the item, then you have unrealized savings because the extra value has not yet been extracted from the transaction. To realize any discount or savings it needs to physically show up at some point as extra cash where it is transferred into something like a savings account. Until this has happened, it is more likely that you have only added to your inventory of stuff. So even though you did not spend as much as you normally would have, this "saving money" activity has only resulted in an outflow of cash and possibly increased your fixed costs of items that you have to maintain.

6. Have you physically taken the cash from the 10%-off that you didn't have to pay into a separate account or place that you never spend? If yes, then you have finally saved money on the purchase; congratulations!

Using the 10% coupon enabled you to consume 10% more than you would have without the coupon—which lowers your cost of living or increases your lifestyle beyond its regular financial capability. To move ahead financially you need to physically set some (or all) of this money aside. This is true for buying anything at a discount or on sale. You may not view saving $5 on dinner as meaningful enough to move to a place of permanent savings, but what if it were $500 on a computer? Or $5,000 on a car? Or $50,000 on a house? Over a lifetime, all of your "saving money" stories that you probably have already could have added up to a significant chunk of money. Savings only occurs if some (or all) of the discount increases your financial stability. The discount must be turned into cash that is permanently set aside somewhere separate for both savings and investments. In these two locations the discount will be generating income to permanently raise your standard of living or giving. Until your savings have been permanently assigned in this manner then its status is uncertain and you are probably not adding to your financial stability.

Winning Concept #3

*Always keep long-term reality in mind; the entire picture.
Since your financial future will occur, wouldn't you like
to know how it is going to play out to make adjustments as
soon as possible?*

It is imperative for you to realize that over your lifetime you are going to earn a *finite* amount of money. Your success in the financial game-of-life hinges on how much of your income that you have available to direct toward your lifetime satisfaction vs. how much you unnecessarily give away (interest charges, poor spending and investing choices, and avoidable taxes) that stunt your spending ability and net worth. The cumulative effect over a lifetime of financially wiser decisions will launch your income and net worth far beyond what it would have been without considering the big picture.

You do not know how long you will live, but you can make a projection. You do not know how much you will earn, but you can make a projection, and each year that you are working it will become more accurate. You can also project large lifetime costs such as housing, transportation, vacations, or events such as weddings or education. You can also predict when you will likely retire and what your income requirements would be. Over the years, your actual income and spending will make your future projections ever more accurate.

It is your goal to keep as much of your lifetime earnings as you can with prudent money management. There are two main tools that you have to defend your pile of lifetime earnings. The first tool is to shield it from unexpected events using insurance for car/health/disability/life/etc. The second tool is spending restraint against institutions (advertisers and taxing authorities trying to grab as much of your lifetime earnings as they can) and then your peer groups that likely want you to join them in activities that you may not be able to afford.

According to the U.S. Census Bureau Surveys 2010, the average lifetime earnings for a high school graduate is $1.2 million; for a college graduate it is $2.1 million and for a Master's degree the average is $2.5 million.[1] This is huge amount of money that is going to be under your control. You have a few ways to manage this money for your benefit:

1. As the manager of your lifetime earnings, are you planning to minimize the taxes on your million in earnings? Why work so hard to earn the money if you are going to give over 50% of it away to various forms of taxes (such as federal income, state income, sales, property, Medicare, social security, and many others.) If you are going to earn $1 million over your lifetime, you are writing a check to the taxing authorities for $500,000. If you could save just 10% of this amount, you would have $50,000 that you could spend according to your values and priorities instead of letting governing authorities decide for you.

2. Are you going to spend this fortune on repeatedly leasing new cars that plummet in value while you are driving them?

3. Are you going to spend most of it on interest charges from continually living above your means with loans and revolving credit card balances?

4. How much of this are you going to save so that you can actually afford to retire at all?

   Don't budget for your next paycheck, budget for a lifetime:
   Lifetime Earnings
   Lifetime Housing
   Lifetime Transportation
   Lifetime Cost of Children
   Lifetime Interest Expense
   Lifetime Education
   Lifetime Donations

Plus your Lifetime Career—which moves will be most advantageous over the next 5 years to position your career for higher earnings?

The next chart shows the average income trajectory by age from the U.S. Census Bureau, Current Population Surveys, March 2000. Although the dollar amounts change every year, the trajectory arc of earnings over time does not. Notice that the income profile of the average wage earner reaches a peak between the ages of 45–55. This is important information: if you only make money from a job, there is a predictable slope of income increases and then decreases over your career. If you are around age 50, it is likely that you are earning the most that you will ever get from wages during your lifetime. The easiest time to save a substantial amount of money is during your peak earning years; if you cannot save during this period your financial goals are going to be very difficult to reach.

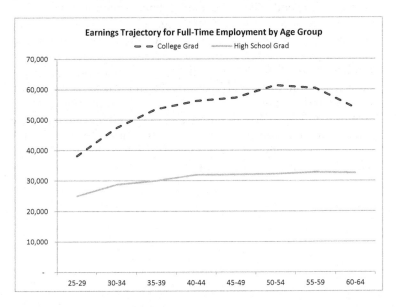

There is a concept of peak lifestyle that needs to correlate with your peak earnings. This is the time when your home, cars, furnishings, vacations, and spending of all types is the most that you will be able to afford from your job. Until your earnings have peaked, most people expect ever-increasing wages and spend correspondingly with the expectation that pay raises and bonuses will continue until you retire. This is possible, but the reality is that this is unlikely. If your lifestyle spending does not match the movements of your level of income, it is likely that you will start a downward spiral of overspending.

For wage earners who do not have a college degree, on average their earnings will have a similar plateau starting around age 42. Just the concept of peak wages reveals how critical it is to have investment income to supplement your earned income.

Although the ideal planning time horizon is a lifetime, start where you can by planning at least 12 months to a few years into the future. As you get in the habit of reviewing your goals and budgets, over time you can extend your planning horizon further and further into the future.

Concept #3 also refers to considering an entire transaction through to the end. There are many business models that exploit incorrect financial decision-making when consumers focus only on one element of a multiple-element transaction. For example, getting a discount on a new car might be a financial step backward if the dealer is giving you a very poor price for trading in your old car. If you are buying an item, have you considered the maintenance costs? If you are replacing an item, have you considered both the sale of the old item, the purchase of the new item along with all of the transition/transfer costs? A free product may not be a good deal if you have to sign an over priced long-term contract.

Winning Concept #4

It is a total delusion that you are free to spend all of your paycheck. Because you must also fund the maintenance and replacement of everything you own.

You cannot spend all of your income because everything physical needs to be maintained and replaced. This includes non-perishable items such as your house, car, boat, appliances, clothing, furniture, and health. As time passes or items are used, everything physical needs repairs or replacement. Where is the money for all of this going to come from if you are already spending all of your money elsewhere? The money to maintain or replace the physical items that you enjoy can only come from your wallet and the most accurate and sustainable time for you to set aside this money is while you are consuming these items. If you cannot afford the ongoing maintenance or the replacement of an item then you simply cannot afford to own that item and should make cheaper arrangements; the sooner the better.

There are real expenses occurring in your life each day—even though you pay for them infrequently. Day by day, physical items are becoming:

1. Worn out (carpeting, car tires, paint, roof, shoes).
2. Depleted (tank of heating oil or propane, firewood).
3. Obsolete (computer software and hardware, mechanical and electronic appliances, sports equipment, fashionable accessories).
4. Plus intangible items are expiring (insurance coverage, registrations, membership fees).

If you are going to create lasting financial stability, then you need to be aware that your daily living and possessions have costs-of-ownership that you have to be able to afford to sustain them in the long run. Life is a never-ending activity of consumption expenses, and Winning Concept #4 is the recognition that you are incurring real financial expenses even when it appears that nothing physical is happening; just the passage of time. These phantom expenses reflect the slow consumption of everything physical that eventually matures to become due and payable by you. So setting aside some money as you consume these items is necessary so that you'll have the money for their predictable maintenance and replacement. These expenses need to be paid by you just to keep your lifestyle the way it is today, and that is why all of your income is not yours to spend.

If you are still not convinced, what do you think happens when you continually do not have enough money for the repairs and replacement of items that wear out, deplete, become obsolete, or expire? Either one of two things will happen: your physical lifestyle starts a downward spiral of disrepair and jury-rigging until it matches the amount of money that you can come up with to spend on a few repairs. Or more troubling, you ignite the financially-dangerous fires of using debt for personal spending for living beyond your means. Although debt is discussed later, continually using debt for these personal expenses are self-inflicted wounds that push you toward financial struggle as you increase your monthly costs. Using debt to live above your means also creates the risk of repossession, foreclosure, bankruptcy, and a poor credit rating.

The means by which you can maintain your current lifestyle is through the obvious concept of constraint or delayed gratification to build a reserve of money to maintain and replace what you own. Many people endure great financial hardships that were foreseeable and avoidable, but they were unwilling to restrain themselves from spending. Although it seems like a big deprivation at the time, it is in fact just reality: if you continually spend all of your income you are guaranteeing that you will never have the reserves of money to maintain your possessions or health. Supporting your life is probably far more expensive than you suspect if you have not mapped out the repair/replacement costs of items that you already own or are planning to purchase.

Winning Concept #5

Money vanishes in weak-financial hands while money piles-up in strong-financial hands.

There is a spectrum of behavioral traits in how people generally act with money-related tasks that I am subjectively labeling Weak to Strong. Weak or strong refer to two points along a spectrum, not permanent traits in opposition to each other. The traits that I list below summarize much of the behavior that I see repeated over and over again with the same financial outcomes. Everyone has these traits in varying degrees and may sporadically move between them. We all begin our financial life with most of the traits of the weak hands and by either personally experiencing the mess they create or learning from others, we start moving a little more toward the traits of a strong-handed money manager.

As a generalization, money vaporizes from the wallets of the weakest-financial hands and accumulates fastest in the wallets of the strongest-financial hands. By reviewing the following table, I hope that you will honestly assess where you repeatedly exhibit the weak-handed traits to see where you could potentially develop a little more toward the strong-handed traits.

Traits of Weak-Financial Hands	Traits of Strong-Financial Hands
1. Impatient and unable to delay any gratification—money ricochets out of your wallet faster than it comes in	1. Patient in making purchases; wait until purchases are affordable and fit into your financial plan

Traits of Weak-Financial Hands	Traits of Strong-Financial Hands
2. Routinely spend more than you can afford for personal pleasure or to create a false public façade of success	2. Impossible to persuade into spending money beyond budgeted amounts or for public perception
3. Unaware of financial concepts or how to apply them to your behavior	3. Operate your life with a sound basis in financial concepts
4. Never discuss personal financial decisions with experts who could help you; put up an iron curtain around personal finance details, not realizing that your financial life is transparent to anyone with a speck of financial knowledge	4. Routinely receive financial advice from people proven to be trustworthy so you may reveal a lot of personal information to get the most accurate advice
5. Surprised by the maintenance costs of things you own, unable to afford their predictable upkeep	5. Predict the total cost of ownership for affordability before purchases are made
6. Shop for the cheapest items you can find, even though over time these can cost more than expensive items that last longer	6. Shop for items with durability; the value of an item over time is more important than an initial low-price; consider the price/usage or price/time rather than just price

Traits of Weak-Financial Hands	Traits of Strong-Financial Hands
7. Buy extraneous stuff prompted by friends, relatives, or coworkers that you never end up using	7. Only buy what is in alignment with your personal values
8. Routinely buy products and services from buddies, relatives, and social acquaintances instead of appropriate or professional experts	8. Only buy products and services from proven professionals with specialized skills that exactly match your current situation; and may become friends built upon successful business transactions
9. No motivation to learn and make informed purchase decisions; afraid to ask for a discount	9. Not afraid to ask confrontational questions before a purchase is made and have questions developed from doing research
10. Allow every financial opportunity to pass by because of a lack of preparation	10. Act instantly on financial opportunities because you are fully prepared and are searching for them
11. Handle financial problems on your own by either guessing or learning from scratch	11. Access a wide range of professional counselors for personal financial matters

Traits of Weak-Financial Hands	Traits of Strong-Financial Hands
12. Expend a lot of time and effort to find a discount on small purchases; waste time bargain-hunting to save tiny dollar amounts	12. Make small purchases quickly at reasonable prices; time is focused on generating more income and becoming more valuable to employers or customers
13. Make large purchases quickly at retail or inflated prices; imprudently overpay by large dollar amounts	13. Make large purchases at wholesale prices; saving large dollar amounts
14. Lack of planning creates financial predicaments that force you to buy and sell large assets at poor prices; no cash or skill to take advantage of market changes or opportunities	14. Have financial reserves and patience to make use of market changes to buy and sell assets at the most favorable prices
15. Consider it normal and acceptable to pay interest on credit card balances, car loans, or still have student debt 5 years after graduation	15. Would never permit a credit card balance to be charged interest or extra fees
16. Repeatedly buy cars with a loan or lease payment when it is inappropriate to do so	16. Every vehicle is always purchased with cash; would never consider a car loan

Traits of Weak-Financial Hands	Traits of Strong-Financial Hands
17. Administrative paperwork is in chaos; missing or incomplete files for legal, financial, insurance, and tax records	17. Legal, financial, insurance, registrations, deeds, and tax records are organized and up to date
18. Incomplete estate planning and documentation that creates unnecessary expenses and chaos among heirs; plans are legally unenforceable, if they exist at all	18. Estate documents and burial plans are complete, legal, and all of the adult beneficiaries are fully informed to minimize drama and expensive lawsuits among heirs
19. Do not consider money to be important or difficult; you simply spend all the money you get your hands on	19. Money is not the most important thing in life, but it does have the greatest impact on every area of your life; consider yourself to be a long-term steward of generational wealth
20. Waste time hoping for a financial windfall or a lucky career break and dream about how to spend it all	20. Consistently follow a self-created financial plan to reach goals
21. Ask other people to co-sign on your loans, or will co-sign for other people (co-signatory is only required when the primary borrower is certain to default)	21. Never co-sign on loans for others or ask others to do so for you; instead, you help them improve a low credit rating

Traits of Weak-Financial Hands	Traits of Strong-Financial Hands
22. Never accept personal blame for the financial consequences of your actions or failure to act—so there is no feedback to improve or do anything different in the future	22. Immediately address financial trouble when it occurs and learn from each instance to avoid it again in the future
23. Have no idea what interest rates you are paying or receiving, do not know the specific terms of your loans or legal contracts	23. Carefully evaluate and monitor all interest rates you are paying and receiving, pay attention to fine print and rule changes
24. Look for the easiest financial solutions that only delay and exacerbate your financial problems	24. Look for financial solutions with long-term sustainability
25. Borrow money for personal spending or routine maintenance; no habit of saving money before purchases are made; repeatedly use the phrase, "I think I can afford this monthly payment"	25. Routinely save to pay cash for all personal spending; there are no circumstances in which you would use debt for personal consumption
26. Publicly show-off money as a big spender or philanthropist	26. Low-key about your financial resources and charitable donations

Traits of Weak-Financial Hands	Traits of Strong-Financial Hands
27. In trying to make a big financial score, you repeatedly make reckless investments that lose your money	27. Only make prudent investments in alignment with your investing capability, that increase your financial stability
28. Ignore or wreck your credit rating and end up paying the highest loan and insurance rates; unable to pass credit checks for employment	28. Maintain an excellent credit rating to access the cheapest personal and business loans, insurance, and career or business opportunities
29. Unable or uncomfortable in saying "No" to people or organizations asking you for money	29. Easily say "No" to people or organizations asking for donations; instead, you follow your own charitable-spending plan in alignment with your personal values
30. Make impulsive decisions with significant financial consequences	30. Disciplined and thoughtful over decisions with financial consequences
31. Intrigued by easy-money schemes when you should be suspicious	31. Refuse to hear about any easy-money or get-rich-quick scheme

Traits of Weak-Financial Hands	Traits of Strong-Financial Hands
32. Will make financial commitments for public appearances; but to the detriment of others, will back out later privately when reality conflicts with your financial ability	32. Thoughtful before making any financial commitment, but then stand by it
33. Repeatedly ask family and friends to bail you out of financial difficulties or support a lifestyle far beyond your means	33. Admit full responsibility and do whatever it takes to get out of financial difficulties
34. During negotiations you react emotionally and are easily offended	34. Diplomatic and respectful in negotiations, always keep your emotions under control
35. Work history is peppered with many industry changes for an easy payoff or whim, with no idea of the long-term career cost of that behavior	35. Career changes are thoughtfully considered only after expending time and effort in researching any new opportunities
36. You are the very last person whom others seek for advice on any financial matter	36. You are the first person whom others seek for advice with their financial affairs

Traits of Weak-Financial Hands	Traits of Strong-Financial Hands
37. Have no idea what a tax strategy is or erroneously believe that your CPA is doing this for you	37. Have a comprehensive tax-reduction strategy; use optimal corporate entities, timing and type of expenses, and classification of investments
38. Leave a trail of financial ruin in your wake through a long list of disappointed relatives, friends, and lenders to whom you still owe money	38. Leave a trail of appreciative supporters by making prompt payments, fair treatment, full disclosure, and have eager financial references
39. Unaware of opportunity costs or minimizing them	39. Seek to discover as many opportunity costs as possible for financial decisions
40. Ignore or procrastinate on financial details that increase the cost of everything you do	40. Immediately handle financial matters as they arise
41. Repeatedly justify overspending by using phrases that focus on immediate gratification, such as "Life is too short," "What good is money if you can't enjoy it," "I've earned it," and everybody's favorite, "I deserve it!" or "You deserve it!"	41. Refrain from overspending using phrases that support financial stability such as "Money doesn't grow on trees," "Never spend money that you don't have," and Benjamin Franklin's classic: "A penny saved is a penny earned"[2]

25

Traits of Weak-Financial Hands	Traits of Strong-Financial Hands
42. Consider it bad etiquette to discuss money, investing, or business during evenings, weekends, meals, vacations, or anytime	42. Available 24/7 when changes in financial circumstances arise and action is needed, readily discuss money matters to help others or to learn
43. Do not have any savings or investments; or a very tiny amount compared to your income peers	43. Routinely add new money to savings, investments, and toward reducing debts
44. Donate so much of your time, effort, and skill to others who ask for help that your own personal matters are left unattended	44. Have set boundaries for donating your time, effort, and skills to prevent being taken advantage of by others
45. A hands-off manager that relies solely on others to complete projects; not involved with the goals, decision-making, guidance, supervision, or feedback (until it is too late to head off expensive disasters)	45. Manage projects with knowledge and advisors, and lead others by providing clear goals, guidelines, follow-up, and feedback
46. Create ambiguous verbal contracts with financial consequences that lead to ruined relationships, or at worst, a date with a judge at the courthouse	46. Agreements are well-defined written contracts with financial consequences to support the respect of each party for a long-lasting relationship

Traits of Weak-Financial Hands	Traits of Strong-Financial Hands
47. Unwilling to pay with money or time for financial advice or investing knowledge, take advice from articles or friends without doing further research	47. Regularly spend money to learn how to get your money and assets working smarter; utilize books, blogs, clubs, newsletters, seminars, advisors, etc.
48. Do not understand how your broker selects investments in your account or how to objectively determine how they are performing	48. Lead your financial advisors with specific goals, regular assessments, and specific triggers to take alternative actions
49. Buy investments after a cold call from a salesperson with a good 'sales story'	49. Only invest with proven managers after performing your due diligence
50. Will not fire advisors when they continually provide substandard performance due to the effort to find a replacement; feel that the relationship with the advisor is not costing you too much money, or not even aware of what standards to apply to their performance	50. Interview advisors thoroughly before they are hired; provide ongoing coaching so that the advisor can meet your needs, but then replace advisors when ongoing needs are not being fulfilled

Traits of Weak-Financial Hands	Traits of Strong-Financial Hands
51. During negotiations, quickly make unreasonable concessions in order to get it over with or be liked by the other party	51. Never concede an unreasonable point during negotiations without getting something of reasonable value in return
52. Avoid hiring people or outsourcing time-consuming tasks that prevent earning more money, or learning to make more money	52. Eager to hire employees or contractors if the time-savings would lead to generating more income; have clear employment policies and increase your financial effectiveness through other people
53. Engage in tax-evasion schemes at the risk of expensive penalties or jail	53. Tax planning and payments are professionally prepared and are conservative with court-tested strategies
54. Have never tracked your spending or net worth to determine where and how to make improvements or trade-offs	54. Regularly track your spending, net worth, and investment performance—along with getting professional advice on how to make improvements

Traits of Weak-Financial Hands	Traits of Strong-Financial Hands
55. The time-horizon for managing your cash flow ranges from having enough money for today to having enough money to last until your next paycheck	55. The time-horizon for managing your cash flow is a minimum of your lifetime and can extend beyond two generations. I know of a family office for wealthy families that plans in 50-year increments
56. Shrug-off money that was lost to fraud and quickly agree to pay financial settlements when you are the victim of frivolous lawsuits	56. Initiate law-enforcement investigations against perpetrators of fraud and legally battle against any frivolous lawsuit
57. Will routinely spend beyond your means for activities to maintain friendships with people who earn far more than you do	57. Never swayed into spending over budget amounts to keep in contact with a social group
58. View prenuptial agreements as unromantic and cynical—but later find yourself the victim of an unfair and expensive divorce judgment	58. View a prenuptial agreement as a collaborative and pragmatic tool for estate planning, insurance and credit rating protection, along with guarding against post-divorce drama. The odds of a divorce are near 50%, and the combined legal fees for both parties in a protracted battle can be the largest single expense of a lifetime

Traits of Weak-Financial Hands	Traits of Strong-Financial Hands
59. Unconcerned whether your children complete high school, vocational training, or college	59. Strive to build an environment where your children would never consider dropping out of high school or college; promote education as the most robust solution for opportunity, employment, income, and achievement
60. Living-in-a-fantasy or denial over your probable future income and expenses	60. Have realistic expectations for future income and expenses
61. Indulge in expensive hobbies or vacations that you cannot afford	61. Do not compromise affordability for anything; save in order to make all purchases with cash
62. Always have excuses to avoid taking steps toward long-term goals	62. Periodically review long-term planning and take concrete steps toward these goals
63. Criticize and complain much more than you compliment and support; diminishing your likelihood of advancement and opportunities from others	63. Compliment and support much more than you criticize and complain; enhancing your likelihood of advancement and opportunities from others
64. Intend to get adequate insurance coverage or update coverage amounts, but never actually do it	64. Regularly assess all kinds of insurance needs and have suitable coverage in force

Traits of Weak-Financial Hands	Traits of Strong-Financial Hands
65. Administrative matters and paperwork are viewed as a hassle to be avoided and minimized; "I'll get around to it sometime"	65. Administrative matters and paperwork are handled diligently and completely; these are sought out because paperwork provides: legal protection, savings, potential profit, tax requirements, plus peace of mind
66. Seek solutions that are cheap, but temporary, which ultimately become far more expensive than a normally-priced solution	66. Seek frugal solutions that are long-lasting
67. Are generous with unappreciative people who continually ask for more money, who use it for lifestyle spending instead of recovering their independence	67. Generous with your effort and resources to temporarily assist others in getting back on their feet
68. Avoid social networking so you do not know where to get assistance to move forward with your career, business, or investment projects	68. Through connecting other people together for their benefit alone, you are able to access people and businesses to move forward on your own projects

Traits of Weak-Financial Hands	Traits of Strong-Financial Hands
69. In business dealings, you do not screen potential customers and end up trying to help clients who cannot be helped, repeatedly work for free by getting taken advantage of, or under-value your service and price it too low	69. In business dealings you screen customers up-front to avoid being played by amateurs, cut out by professionals, or stabbed in the back by competitors
70. Consume all of your free time and money on leisure, entertainment, or maintenance	70. Ratchet down the amount of empty entertainment in your life to make room for activities that are financially productive; self-motivated to accomplish goals
71. Do not educate yourself enough to determine whether you are getting good advice or bad advice	71. Do not hesitate to learn, and use skeptical questions to determine whether you are getting good advice or bad advice
72. Do not have goals for your life beyond some extra leisure activities, find yourself getting bored	72. Have several long-term goals including a few of which that may not be completed in a lifetime
73. Give up when told that your new business idea will not amount to anything by family, friends, or co-workers	73. Ignore others' casual opinions about your projects or goals

Traits of Weak-Financial Hands	Traits of Strong-Financial Hands
74. Routinely, an early adopter of new gadgetry and pay extra to be among the first to get a new model as soon as it comes out	74. Wait for prices to drop on new products; watch to see which technologies succeed so you do not load up on dead-end product platforms
75. Self-sabotage by imagining reasons to give away money and property to others that you cannot afford to lose	75. Help others with time, effort, and money; but do not take ownership of other peoples' problems to solve for them
76. Ignore repeated pleas from your friends, relatives, or accountant that your spending is out of control or that you are taking on too much debt	76. Have determined exactly what level of spending is affordable using financial principles; seriously consider unsolicited advice from others when it is the same concern from many independent sources
77. Routinely lie to your partner (or parents if younger), about how much money you earn, spend, and particularly, how much debt that you owe	77. Transparent with your partner (or parents if younger), about spending and debts, and resolve all disagreements about money matters
78. Not comfortable with risk, so you avoid all investing, which eliminates the possibility for financial growth	78. Accept investment risks, but manage them with education and active participation

Traits of Weak-Financial Hands	Traits of Strong-Financial Hands
79. Hoard all savings in the form of cash or gold buried in your backyard, because you do not trust banks, currencies, or courts; consider living "off the grid"	79. May have some emergency cash at home, but operate normally to increase your savings, investments, and businesses. (Protect against catastrophic economic changes by diversifying among currencies, countries, and using financial hedges)
80. Never contribute in any way to the charity of others by giving with your time, money, effort, goods, or skill	80. A regular contributor to others that may include volunteering time, money, effort, goods, skill, or connecting other people together
81. A prickly personality that over-reacts to small disagreements and frequently elevates them to law enforcement or a date at small claims court (only to lose many of your cases)	81. An agreeable person who finds ways to build goodwill, mitigate conflict, and resolve disagreements amicably
82. The value of your possessions unnecessarily plummets from neglectful care, unprofessional repairs, misuse, and a lack of warranty or insurance to fix normal and expected usage	82. The value of your possessions remains high due to attentive care, preventative maintenance, professional repairs, and appropriate insurance coverage

Traits of Weak-Financial Hands	Traits of Strong-Financial Hands
83. Do not live extravagantly and cannot figure out why you have so little money to spend	83. Aware of financial concepts and track your finances to prevent problems and address concerns
84. Have a mortgage with a term that will last into retirement or even beyond your expected lifespan	84. Make certain that your home mortgage is scheduled to be paid off before any probable retirement date
85. Do not map out meals or food comparison pricing; erroneously believe that fast food is a cheap way to feed your family to justify how frequently you go there for an easy meal	85. Meals are planned days or weeks in advance to take advantage of efficient food buying and getting broad nutrition
86. Reach too far for the dream home, vacation house, or yacht, but end up: broke because it was unaffordable from the start; divorced due to the stress on an already fragile and strained family; or demoted/fired because of all the time cutting into work hours spent enjoying or managing the newly-expanded lifestyle	86. Expensive "dream" purchases must be easily affordable, and significant lifestyle changes are only made if there is capability in place that will not diminish family quality-of-life or career prospects

Traits of Weak-Financial Hands	Traits of Strong-Financial Hands
87. Spend money from retirement accounts before retiring because it is expedient instead of scrambling to find additional income as if it were a crisis; find it acceptable to use the phrase "dip into savings"	87. Defend retirement assets and all categories of money from ever being spent on something other than their purpose; would *never consider* prematurely withdrawing money from retirement accounts
88. In the workplace, renowned for being the biggest slacker, most inflexible complainer, or drama-queen/king victim	88. In the workplace, renowned for being the most valuable, reliable, capable, emotionally level, best at learning new things, and willing to head up new projects
89. Make flippant bets on investment ideas without thoroughly researching them. For example, "I saw that XYZ was down to $1 a share so I put $5,000 into it; they are a well-known brand and should never be that low"; months before the company declares bankruptcy	89. Investments are only made in areas in which you have great knowledge, expertise, and investment insight; otherwise you directly manage those who have proven they are capable at doing this for you

Traits of Weak-Financial Hands	Traits of Strong-Financial Hands
90. Become a jellyfish around confrontation and never stand up for yourself or others; or are too confrontational over minor transgressions	90. Although always diplomatic in dealing with others, you have a will of steel to stand up for yourself and others; never afraid of any confrontation, but battles are chosen very judiciously and are slowly elevated to a firmer stance
91. Avoid all stressful tasks such as public speaking, interviewing, making a cold call, long application forms, performing with others watching, distant travel, administrative hurdles	91. Seek anxiety-producing events that most people shy away from because all achievement and greater success is on the other side of these events
92. When a goal appears to be difficult, you quickly give up and make excuses; spend a lot of time talking about your bad luck or lost opportunities instead of moving forward on them	92. If a goal appears to be too challenging, you: ask for assistance, get creative, and put in more time and effort to persist until you ultimately get the results that you are seeking
93. Make expensive purchases with no thought of all the long-term consequences of owning something unaffordable	93. Expensive decisions are examined for their impact to your net worth; evaluate by determining if this choice will consume or contribute to your net worth over time

Traits of Weak-Financial Hands	Traits of Strong-Financial Hands
94. Dodge all responsibility and blame others for your own financial failures and problems	94. Seek responsibilities knowing that the more you take on, the more you will be rewarded and the more experience you will accumulate
95. Cling to a career in a dying company, industry, geographic region, or country long after it is clear that opportunities will continually diminish in the future	95. Seek careers in a growth company, industry, geographic region, or country to maximize opportunities for skill development, salary, and potential investment opportunities
96. All unexpected income is spent immediately	96. Extra income is permanently set aside and added to the bankroll, only some of its earnings are spent, *never* the principal amount
97. Throw in the towel on ambition and look for permanent handouts from the government or others for whom this is not their responsibility	97. Never stop exploring new careers, projects, business opportunities and investments
98. Think your money problems would be solved if you could just get a little extra salary	98. Minimize money problems with financial stability and investment income

Traits of Weak-Financial Hands	Traits of Strong-Financial Hands
99. Affordability is solely determined by how much money is in your pocket or checking account right now; or worse, your credit card limit	99. Affordability is determined by a detailed long-term financial map of your income, spending, savings, and investing plan
100. Even though savings and retirement accounts are underfunded or non-existent, most of your variable spending goes to restaurants, shopping, bars, electronics, or travel	100. Some time or money is used for discovering new income-producing investments to drive up your investment income
101. Erroneously rely on your employer to give you professional challenges and fulfillment, along with an ever increasing salary and benefits	101. Use employment earnings to fund investment income and a side business for ever-increasing earnings and challenges; the sooner you wean yourself from employment as your sole income source, the sooner you will gain more financial self-determination
102. Mismanagement of credit cards piles up expensive fees, penalties, and cash-flow problems	102. Prudent use of credit cards, that are paid off in full every month, is a monthly source of financial benefits: cash back, points, miles, or leveraging low interest-rates

Traits of Weak-Financial Hands	Traits of Strong-Financial Hands
103. Live paycheck-to-paycheck during your peak earning years (age 45–55)	103. Utilize your peak earning years to save the most amount of monthly money toward financial goals
104. Naively get an adjustable-rate mortgage only to be predictably forced out of your home when mortgage rates leap up beyond what is affordable to your income	104. Residential mortgages are always at a fixed-rate and are refinanced when rates drop by enough that you are not extending the life of your mortgage when you apply the monthly savings to the outstanding balance
105. Do not want to manage your own investments, so you turn it all over to a financial advisor who continually loses money and under-performs the market averages	105. Oversee and regularly monitor both investments and advisors
106. Have never planned your day or week, let alone a decade or your lifespan; no rush to accomplish any goal or become more efficient and productive	106. A desperate sense of urgency not to waste time, not a single moment to spare in being productive; crazy-obsessive and relentless about advancing toward your goals every day

Traits of Weak-Financial Hands	Traits of Strong-Financial Hands
107. Avoid learning for the workplace and dodge being challenged in your career	107. A sponge in learning new things in and around your career; when your work challenge slows (increasing responsibility or skills), you immediately hunt for a new job or project that will provide more challenge and increase your value to others
108. Have never had a thought about wealth building beyond a lucky lottery ticket	108. Have a plan for wealth that includes adding to your net worth every time you receive any income
109. Focus on the cost of travel arrangements instead of the time lost or the cost of hiring out normal maintenance instead of how much productive time you are throwing away by doing things yourself	109. Purchase "time" to have more productive time for making money; (hire out maintenance like housekeeping, yard work, and increase your speed of travel from slower methods to something faster)
110. Inherited property is eventually seized for non-payment of taxes or loans; inherited vehicles fall into disrepair until they are junked	110. Inherited property is maintained or sold to maximize its value

Traits of Weak-Financial Hands	Traits of Strong-Financial Hands
111. Apply for retirement social security benefits as early as possible, locking in the lowest possible payment schedule for decades	111. Delay your application for social security retirement benefits for a few years to increase your monthly payment by up to 75% for decades to come
112. Hold onto unused jewelry and expensive toys that gather dust, become dated, or obsolete as they depreciate in value	112. Unused assets are quickly sold, bartered, donated, or gifted to capture or give as much value as possible
113. Do not adjust your spending for changes in your income or fixed-expenses that lead to over spending and under saving	113. Use ratios for money management that automatically adjust to changes in your income
114. Forced to sell some of your stuff for cents-on-the-dollar to pay for predictable bills that you cannot afford	114. Anticipate income and expenses months ahead to manage them in the most advantageous manner
115. Compound investments downward with losses and spending the principal; compound debts upward with new debt and higher interest rates	115. Utilize upward compounding to increase investment income and compound debt balances downward to zero

Traits of Weak-Financial Hands	Traits of Strong-Financial Hands
116. Avoid getting a job or making money in high school or college, take a year off of college or during your work career; quit a job before finding another one	116. Sprint directly toward career goals and financial ambitions, always building on the momentum of earlier career advancement and skill development, "upward and onward"; would never allow a career to stall or miss an opportunity to move forward
117. Rely on hope or fate that things will improve or change for the better	117. Rely on action to advance toward goals
118. Focus solely on an investment's potential gain or yield and ignore all of the risks	118. Focus first on all of an investment's risks and the return of your principal; only when satisfied do you consider the potential gain
119. Career advancement or change is stalled by the tiniest obstacles, or even imaginary ones, by guessing about what may be difficult	119. All career planning and changes are thoroughly researched, plus you get further career advice from people who are actually working in the position

Traits of Weak-Financial Hands	Traits of Strong-Financial Hands
120. Decide to have children with no idea about all of the immediate and long-term costs; no plan to create the income to cover all of the predictable expenses of having children	120. Before choosing to have children, map out the income needed to cover the cost of the birth, child-care, possibility of one parent leaving work or changing to part-time, health insurance, as well as clothing, toys, camps, braces, projects, sports equipment, musical instruments, transportation, electronics, college, etc. for each child
121. Gritless about financial matters that would lower your costs or increase your income	121. Have tremendous resilience regarding financial matters, in spite of any adversity, to optimize your finances
122. Focus on, think about, and talk about how to increase your *salary and employee benefits* as your two most important financial assignments	122. Focus on, think about, and talk about how to increase your *investment income and net worth* as your two most important financial assignments

Although most of these traits are obvious, notice that: whenever something has needlessly cost you extra money, it was when you were following the weak-handed traits and whenever you benefited (or were protected from losses) was when you were following the strong-handed traits. The themes running through the traits of strong-handed money managers are: putting your focus on reality, planning for your future, acting thoroughly and professionally, and learning for a lifetime. These themes are necessary in the financial game-of-life if you want to change your position from being the patsy to being the player. Another label for weak and strong hands is financially ineffectual and financially proficient. To move from the weak side to the strong side many of the traits just require awareness, but some also require willpower and discipline to perform them or keep them up as ongoing habits.

Do not be disappointed if you have a few, many, or most of the traits of weak-handed money managers because, as was mentioned, we all start in this position when we have no guidance. It is only through our own experiences or anecdotal stories from others that we patch together a few financial ideas. Whenever a financial mistake is made it can serve to clarify where you need to make an improvement. You do not have to exhibit all of the traits of the strong-handed people in order to have financial stability, but you do have to move away from as many of the weak-handed traits as possible. Each of the traits can have a critical impact on your finances and life; please learn from the numerous people who have already made these mistakes.

For others who may already have many or all of the strong-handed traits, there are other advanced levels on the money-management spectrum (but these demand entrepreneurial effort and more persistence than most people are willing to expend). Two groups that I will only mention are the Money Magnets (exemplified by Apple company founder Steve Jobs and Virgin company founder Richard Branson) and the Financial Emperors (exemplified by self-made tycoon Li Ka-shing). At this level, there can be a temptation to be greedy to the detriment of others. When movies stereotype those who are greedy, they are referring to a group that you need to stay away from, the traits of Iron-Fists-with-Spikes (exemplified by the character Mr. Potter in the Christmas movie, "It's a Wonderful Life"; or by the character Ebinezer Scrooge in Charles Dickens' book, *A Christmas Carol)*.

The long-term effect of the weak-handed or strong-handed traits builds up to create sharply divergent lifestyles and net worth for people with the same income, experience, or capability. People exhibiting many of the weak-handed traits spend their lives in financial crisis and are rarely able to retire without being subsidized by others. Meanwhile, people exhibiting many of the strong-handed traits have more freedom from all kinds of financial constraints and are likely to have the option to retire comfortably before the age of 60.

You may have also noticed there are industries that solely target the weak-handed money managers: expensive check-cashing fees for those without bank accounts, loans with very high rates from pawn shops, payday lenders, title lenders, and then collection agencies, repo towing, lottery sellers, and expensive debit and credit cards, to name a few. Those who cannot or will not manage their money end up transferring it to those who do manage their money.

People tend to have the most conflict with others who are on the opposite side of the weak/strong spectrum. The difference in perception is similar to an old George Carlin joke about driving a car: anyone driving slower than you is annoyingly holding you up, and anyone driving faster than you is acting reckless. Naturally, whatever speed that you are driving is the only correct one. In the case of these psychological traits, a weak-handed person assesses the strong-handed person as a meddling control-freak, too financially conservative, cynical, and an overbearing micromanager. Their stereotypical image of strong-handed people would be that of a crusty old penny-pincher quick to judge others as spendthrifts, greedy to take advantage of others, who miss out on all of life's joys and want to prevent others from spending money and enjoying life. Contrarily, a strong-handed person assesses the weak-handed person as overly self-indulgent with irresponsible habits, financially naïve, and childishly short-sighted. Their stereotypical image would be that of a spoiled trust-fund kid, with no appreciation for the sacrifice that created the money, lavishly spending themselves into bankruptcy, oblivious to the unnecessary hardships that they are creating for themselves along with all the people who care for or rely on them. Neither of these opinions is likely to be fully accurate, but it may help you to be aware of how people on different parts of the spectrum experience and judge each other; whether openly or in private.

Other Psychological Landmines

There is a psychological conflict between knowing some financial principles vs. human nature (to succumb to immediate gratification, procrastination, and following the path-of-least-resistance). Let the next ideas help add weight to your financial knowledge to counter-balance ingrained habits that are not in your best interest.

While insurance is financial protection from an unexpected single event, there is a self-inflicted danger that you cannot insure: Splurge Syndrome. Any hole in a boat below the waterline will inevitably cause it to sink. Similarly, it only takes a single financial weakness, on a repeated basis, to develop into an unsustainable financial crisis. Benjamin Franklin wrote, "Beware of little expenses for a small leak can sink a great ship."[2] We normally think of a severe addiction to drugs or gambling that can consume a family's income and assets; but a financial leak can truly come from anything. Whenever the desirability of buying something now is more important than the financial consequences later, you've passed the threshold into the splurge syndrome. As an example, let's say that someone has strong financial hands in every area except for one, they collect antique clocks. Now there is nothing wrong with antique clocks or having a large collection of them. But when someone is compelled to buy antique clocks when they cannot afford them, they have a dangerous hole below the metaphorical waterline in their wallet, and are heading into financial trouble. We all have things that we like to have, or buy, or attend, but when an item is so desirable that you buy it repeatedly when you cannot afford it, your indulgence is going to put your financial boat at risk. Everybody spends money differently but it is by monitoring your financial situation that you become alerted to financial weaknesses before they develop into a crisis. Leaks that are continuing to drain your wallet will create a large lifetime deficit from your financial optimum.

The Splurge Syndrome also applies to companies. A family friend is a business turnaround consultant for family-held companies. She says that the majority of the time her services are requested from the third-generation of the business founder. The founder (with strong-hands) builds a successful business and the second-generation coasts on this success, and was mentored by the founder. But by the third generation (weak-hands), the business has so many bloated expenses and non-contributing family members on the payroll that only outside experts can save the business from so many forms of overspending.

By following the principles and rules in this book, you are going to have access to a lot more money in the months and years to come. As your accounts grow, you are likely to bump into several psychological challenges:

1. Your increasing capacity to spend and borrow will make it possible to create large financial problems, if you are so tempted. Pent up demand for items long-coveted may overwhelm prudent spending, or you may qualify for a large debt that can consume too much of your income.

2. Self-sabotage can cause reckless spending and investing that prevents increasing your financial stability. Having significantly more money than your relatives or peers can cause emotional or social discomfort that is then relieved by "losing" this extra money in some way. Breaking landmark numbers for age or salary ($50,000; $100,000) or savings ($10,000; $100,000) may elicit beliefs about money that you were unaware of previously. For an example: some people believe that they have "financially arrived" by reaching a magic salary level of say, $100,000. They then start believing that at this level of success they should be able to afford anything that they want—and triggering this belief allows them to start spending more than their income. Or someone reaches a certain age and believes that they should at least be able to afford X by this age, no matter what their financial situation. Being aware of this phenomenon may help you notice that you have something to work on. The reality is that an increasing amount of spending will subsume any level of income. Even with a low income we can commit some self-sabotage by using the excuse that "I've got nothing to lose," or "it will never add up to anything" and spend what little there is on lottery tickets or knickknacks instead of financial stability.

3. Your larger account balances are going to attract an increasing number of people who want your money: relatives, friends, skilled salespeople, charities, start-up entrepreneurs, hospital administrators, clergy, con artists, professional plaintiffs, and politicians. I once read a study on people living in low income areas who had no savings and one of the reasons they cited for the lack of savings was social pressure. Whenever he or she accumulated a little money, family, relatives, and friends would hound them for a loan that is never repaid. So it was possible for them to save but it was impossible to keep it in an environment that does not support financial stability. You can help neutralize this problem by carefully choosing with whom you discuss any financial matters; strengthening your resolve to increase your financial stability; clarifying your spending values; and possibly changing your environment.

4. Your equanimity will be tested when there are possibilities for making or losing amounts of money that are much larger than you are accustomed to experiencing. You may become paralyzed in moving forward with financial decisions or be unable to sleep with the financial risks that you have taken. You may recklessly invest in something that you know little about as you were too eager to finally have enough money to access investments with large minimum amounts. You can help to increase your composure by exposing yourself to dollar amounts far larger than you are planning, by using ratios or other reference points with which you are familiar, or by increasing your level of knowledge until you discover for yourself that a particular investment is a prudent financial decision.

As a simple exercise, think of the most expensive single investment that you have ever made, and then keep adding a zero to that dollar amount until the thought of investing that much of your money becomes uncomfortable for you. For example, maybe buying a bank certificate of deposit of $1,000 for 5 years is no big deal to your current psychology. Imagine adding another zero and then another, then another; keep adding zeros—of your hard-earned money that you have diligently accumulated. You may notice that at some point your thoughts will start firing off, "Whoa, that is too much of my money in one place! I better make sure that the bank's credit is good! I wonder if this is the best rate I can get? Is 5 years too long; should I get a shorter term? Someone said a CD is a horrible investment so maybe I shouldn't..." So you've built up some savings with discipline but notice that you still become psychologically rattled about what to do with your money when nothing but another zero has been added.

5. Another social factor affecting your financial stability is the financial capability of the people with whom you spend the most time. The desire to belong to a group of people that you enjoy and respect is a powerful psychological force; particularly to people who are young. People unwittingly model the people that they are around the most, so you need to watch your own financial capability more closely when you are involved with a peer group whose income is very different than your own. No one admits to "Keeping up with the Joneses," but continual exposure to others' behavior is the mechanism by which this occurs.

There is an extra psychological challenge to be close friends with a group of people who are far above or far below your level of income. When you want to accompany friends who earn a lot more, you are far more likely to overspend your budget on activities that they can easily afford: a favorite expensive restaurant, another expensive vacation, an expensive hobby, or buying clothing and accessories beyond your budget because you want to fit in with the group. These choices create continual overspending to support relationships that you cannot financially sustain. Your financial stability is also at risk when the group of people with whom you spend a lot of time earn far less than you do. In this case your psychological risk is becoming the group's financial benefactor. Since "you are rich" and "have all this extra money," you frequently end up picking up the tab for activities, putting dinner on your credit card (they say they will pay you back but never do), putting up the deposit for rental vehicles, vacation spots, etc., and are accepting the financial risk for their damages. They may view your higher earning ability as unfair, or lucky, or believe that if you have more money than others then you should continually share it or you are being too selfish. Whatever the justification, I frequently see money transfer from a generous person with means to their unappreciative relatives and ungrateful friends with less income, who ask for

more and keep expecting more of it until it is all gone.
Other points about the people you spend the most time
around:

- Do they focus on opportunity or victimhood?
- Do they learn and try new things or do the
  same old thing?
- Are their incomes going up sharply or are they
  flat/declining?
- Are they effective in moving forward on their
  goals or just interesting talkers?
- In how many ways do you match these people?
- Are they where you want to be in five years?
- Can you find one person to spend time with
  that is a little closer to where you want to be?

The last element of emotions around money is: to accept
that financial ambition will also result in a few financial bruises
along the way. Some will be your own mistakes, while others
will be due to little or no fault of your own. These are going
to be big hits to your net worth and can be equally devastating
to your personal relationships and self-esteem. Your first
reaction is to retreat, hide, keep it a secret, and then never do
X again. The entire list of weak-handed traits is from common
missteps, but any time you lose money is a great financial
learning moment. To recoil is the normal emotional reaction.
But it is my recommendation that you do not recoil in any
way; you must find a way to the other side of your painful
feelings when losses occur until you do not take it personally
and whither. You will be all the wiser for your next financial
trial and perhaps develop some better decision-making criteria
for yourself. But you need to get back into the game of life to
move your financial life forward. I do not know a financially
successful person who hasn't made several financial mistakes.
I once had a greedy moment and violated one of my own
investing rules. The result was a sharp loss on a trade that
lasted only 15 seconds. Believe me; these rules are now seared
in my mind and iron-clad. Lessons that are hard-learned add
to my discipline and grit when I am tempted by either greed or
fear. Most people hunker down and retreat at their first notable
loss. Those with financial ambition refine their money rules

and move forward to their next financial move without getting stuck in the past. Have you made any broad limiting decisions based on a financial loss in your past?

It is normal to fear a career setback, an investment loss, or a start-up business that fails. But the highest financial success is reserved only for those who go beyond their fear and prudently continue to take risks with their career, investing, and businesses. Doing it over and over, learning, failing, networking, refining rules, but always moving forward on opportunities is the path forward to financial success. The richest people that I have met continually take risk and are very comfortable in new situations where most people are not. This allows them to ratchet up their activities to their next level of success.

Winning Concept #6

Incurring debt for personal consumption is forbidden and must be permanently extinguished from your life.

It does not matter whether you have any personal debt or how much it might be, but you must make the commitment: never borrow money for personal expenses *ever again*. If you currently have personal debts, just chip away at paying them down until they are gone; even if you need to create extra income to do so.

There are many purposes for debt but all of them can be placed into one of 5 categories for financial decision-making; and each one will be discussed in detail. You can use debt to purchase:

1. *Personal items or services*—this is financial self-mutilation; which could grow into financial ruin.
2. *College or Trade education*—limited debt based on your expected career income at a reasonable fixed-rate is a wise move that can sharply improve your earnings capability over your lifetime. As such, this debt is considered an investment to increase your lifetime earning potential.
3. *Home*—a mortgage is rent-substitution that must be affordable to your level of income; allows you to minimize your housing cost through slowly eliminating your mortgage balance over time.
4. *Investments that produce predictable cash income*—a good strategy if approached and managed in a professional manner with full-time, up to date, professional-level knowledge and follow-through. Even with this in place, the debt must be limited to an amount that you can afford to pay back in less than 2 years if the investment fails from its first moment. (This category and the next function as a debt but they are actually capital infusions for a business activity to produce an investment return).
5. *Investments solely for capital gain*—a potential catastrophe unless: you are extremely knowledgeable, highly

Financial Literacy

experienced, and have cash reserves with a high cash flow to easily and quickly repay the entire loan if the investment fails. But even with these, it is risky behavior that should be limited to a very small percentage of your portfolio.

1. Personal Expenses

A personal item bought for consumption with interest-bearing debt is the exact opposite of wealth creation. Personal debt created in this manner should be more accurately labeled as negative savings, reverse compounding, or permanent wealth destruction because it guarantees a financial loss for the debtor. For example, a secured loan is a transaction that turns part of an illiquid asset into spendable money for a fee. If you were to own a car free-and-clear and then take out a loan for half of its value, you are, in effect, selling half of the car to make that portion of its value liquid to spend. You are then obligated by the loan to buy back that half of the car you sold at a premium price by paying back the principal loan amount plus interest. So you are selling half of your car at a low price and buying it back at a higher price, which always guarantees a loss on this transaction. This small loss represents the best-case scenario for a loan. If you are unable to repay the loan on time, you lose 100% of the vehicle through repossession even though you sold and only received money for 50% of the car. Each and every personal loan creates a loss from selling low and buying high. How many of these losing transactions would you like to have? How many of these losing transactions can you afford? How many of these losing transactions can your net worth sustain in the worst-case scenario? How much money have you already obliterated in interest and fees by doing these? Even one of these losing transactions creates a permanent financial deficit between where you are today and where you could have been.

Many of you are thinking that a little debt is not a big deal. So let me explain further: when you pay interest on personal loans you have increased your monthly expenses by the interest charges. This is an extra fixed-expense that is making you poorer than you would have been for every month that you allow it to occur. The interest payment that you are now obligated to pay turns money that you have earned into money you can never spend. Interest on personal debt reduces the amount of your money available for current consumption, prolongs the amount of time it takes to save up for larger purchases, and reduces the amount available for your long-term financial stability. The result of paying for these little interest charges creates a permanent and inescapable drop in your lifestyle—you have less money to spend because more of your income is going to your lenders. If you live above your means today by using credit, it is a mathematical necessity that you have to live much further below your means tomorrow to pay it back.

Here is some of the illogic that is at play when you borrow for personal consumption: When you realize that you cannot afford something with cash, how is it somehow affordable to go ahead and buy it anyway at a higher price by piling up interest charges? How you already manage your finances could not build up enough money for the original purchase, but now that this amount is on a credit card, the purchase price—plus all of the interest that will accrue—will magically appear? The average interest charge for personal items doubles the cost of the original item by the time it is fully paid off. So by the time you payoff what you have charged, you have paid for the item twice! It is a financial mirage that you can afford these items with debt and pay them off over time. The cumulative loss of wealth over your lifetime by repeatedly engaging in this behavior will include many zeros in the amount.

Those explanations are the basic theories against personal debt. In real life, the true danger of personal debt is a cascade that I call "unknowingly pulling the pin on the debt-grenade." All debts require discipline in cash-flow timing to make each and every payment on time. Each payment due is a new test for putting the pin back into the grenade before it blows up your finances and credit rating. For example, let us suppose that you bought a car with a $15,000 car loan. Remember that all personal loans raise your fixed costs and thus make you poorer. In a debt cascade scenario, let us say that you have made the payments for a couple months, and it is financially tighter than you expected. Then you realize that you have two unexpected bills to pay, there is no food for your family tomorrow, and you still do not have enough money for the car payment. So you add a personal loan to tide you over until your next paycheck (creating more interest charges that further increases your fixed costs), and then pay only the minimum balance on your credit cards (which maintains your high interest charges and fixed costs). In the worst case, this debt snowballs out of control until you are insolvent. When you cannot pay the monthly minimum on all of your debt, you have failed to put all of the debt pins you are juggling back into place and your debt-grenades start exploding. It can take a few months or many years—but you unknowingly setup this predictable financial damage at the first purchase with personal debt that was not affordable.

Many people incur personal debts and keep them small enough that they are not in danger of financial difficulty. But this is still a big financial mistake. When you can afford your debt obligations, it is still a financial-stability failure similar to lighting your cash on fire. The fire continues to consume the cash straight from your wallet until it is paid off. If you are not carefully monitoring your finances, the fire can spread out of control and burn through all of your money, and more. In the most favorable scenario, if you monitor your fire of debt and keep it under control, you are still making yourself poorer and falling further from your lifetime-financial trajectory. Each dollar that you burn in interest expense represents money that you earned but can never spend, save, invest, or donate.

The concept of financial compounding works on both sides of every personal-consumption loan: one party is getting increasingly richer from receiving the payments (the lender) and the other party is becoming poorer by making the interest payments (the borrower). One side is adding to their financial stability while the other side is reducing their financial stability and making their financial goals more difficult. Paying interest charges for personal expenses is money that is pre-consumed before you receive it; it is eating tomorrow's lunch today and relying on hope that you will always be able to repeat this routine for tomorrow's lunch. Years from now you cannot look at your wallet and actually see all of the missing $100 bills in interest payments that you could have built into a substantial amount of money. But the huge reduction in your current and future net worth *is* the financial reality.

When you are shopping and interested in making a large purchase with a payment plan, if you utter these words, "I just want to know how much is the monthly payment?" The salesperson knows that they are about to get a nice commission because within that phrase are several hidden messages. You are communicating to the salesperson that:

- You can charge me any interest rate you want because I don't spend the time to understand interest-rate charges.
- Even with a teaser 0% interest rate, you can charge me a higher price than normal because it will be hidden among a monthly payment where I cannot easily comparison shop. I won't worry about the date when the teaser-interest rate ends and the contract changes to a sky-high interest rate.
- You can stretch the payments out for a very long time because I do not add up all the interest I pay, I only care if I have enough money each month to make a payment for a month or two.
- I am probably not a careful money manager so you better overcharge me on warranties/ treatments/other fees to make a quick profit since I might not be able to make all of my payments.

There are successful lenders making a lot of money targeting people who use the phrase, "Just tell me how much the monthly payment is." Don't ever let this be you! For cars, homes, TVs, boats, furniture, the salesperson sees dollar signs when a customer says those words. Contrast that phrase to a question that a better money manager would ask of a salesperson, "I've been to several stores to compare features and options, your model isn't exactly the one I want, but what would be your best cash price if I bought this one right now?" In this case, here are the underlying messages that they are communicating to the salesperson:

- Do not give me an inflated price because I'll know it instantly.
- I make careful, educated financial decisions so I'll need thorough responses from you to move forward with a purchase.

- I want to buy, but I am in no hurry. So if you want to make a sale right now, you have to give me your lowest price.
- There is no possibility to hide any interest charges from me.
- Any extra options need to be itemized for me to carefully evaluate.

A consequence of using debt for a personal expense is that this becomes a habit; a costly one that erodes your net worth if done on a continual basis. Habits are hard to break and there are no warning labels on debt that indicate how much you are stunting your financial growth and eroding your financial stability.

What about an offer for a 0%-interest loan on a purchase; isn't that a good thing? I can give you 4 reasons why even this type of transaction is a mistake: it is highly probable that the item is overpriced, you are reinforcing your appetite for instant gratification on items that you cannot afford, you are reinforcing the bad habit to buy items with payments over time, and if you cannot afford to buy the item with cash, you are spending money that you have not yet earned, making the item susceptible to repossession and a total financial loss for you. There is only one situation where 0% interest is a favorable transaction: when you actually have all of the money necessary to make the entire purchase up front, you have shopped around to make sure it is a great price, and you read the fine print to avoid any extra fees and charges that may apply. In this case only, you can set all the money aside for the purchase someplace where it earns interest for you and then withdraw it as needed to make the 0%-loan payments on time. I know someone who bought a car with so many different discounts that she ended up getting 31% off of the list price. Part of this discount was generated by using the funds to purchase the car to invest at 4% while borrowing money from the car company at 0%.

When people in financial trouble ask me for help there are generally three main causes. First, their debts are far too high for their income; expenses like the mortgage, car payments, boat payments, and a home cleaning service are starving them in other areas. Second, they spend too much money for their income on entertainment (dining out, vacations, concerts, barhopping, piles of electronic gadgets, plus expensive alcohol to enjoy with all of the above). A corresponding problem with a high level of entertainment spending is buying all the accessories to fit in socially—clothing, jewelry, shoes, watches, hairstyles, home furnishings, gifts, etc. The third main cause for financial trouble, and the rarest in my experience, is an unexpected tragedy, either health-related expenses or a prolonged loss of employment. Insurance does not cover all types of health problems and there is little assistance for long-term unemployment. Each of these three major problems can cause people to start borrowing far more money than their income can support and unfortunately they call me for help only when a financial collapse is imminent.

Debt to Purchase Vehicles

Owning a car is a necessity for many families. How you choose to acquire that car will dramatically affect your net worth. There is no unique debt aspect to buying a car—it is just another personal debt and a financial mistake. Set aside 4-8% of your income and assign it to a transportation/vehicle reserve and buy a car whenever this reserve is large enough to pay the entire price of the vehicle that you want. A car loan is a personal debt that needlessly increases your monthly fixed costs. Unlike an investment, vehicles are consumed with use or time. When you drive a new car off the dealer's lot it loses 11% of its value; and any 5 year-old car is worth crumbs compared to its original purchase price (only 37% of its original price).[3] When you purchase any car, the amount of money that you are annually consuming is equal to the car's drop in value each year. When you borrow money to buy a car you are simultaneously increasing your fixed expenses with interest payments and reducing your net worth by the amount of money that the car drops in value. Both of these behaviors are the opposite of adding to your wealth, and doing this repeatedly throughout your lifetime transfers a fortune from your wallet into the hands of the automotive finance companies.

Getting a car through a leasing plan is financially worse than a car loan: not only are you limiting your ownership of the car to its sharpest drop in value (the first few years), you are paying interest and a host of fees to do so. You are also paying sales tax on the maximum value of the car and dividing it over the fewest number of years because you have to do it again within only a couple years for the next lease. Do not forget other joys of lease contracts such as the mileage penalty, early termination fee, damage deposit, and a down payment that will have a fancy name such as capital-acquisition-fee or capital-cost-reduction-fee. Leases also create a very expensive problem when your circumstances change for the type of vehicle you need but you are locked into a contract for years. A leased car also restricts your timeframe for replacing your car, giving you a purchasing window where you are least able to maneuver to get the car model, features, or timing that would offer you the best value.

Of course, there are circumstances where lease or rental is the best financial option for car ownership. This is when your need for a vehicle has circumstances limited to a defined period of time plus you have determined that by comparing the cost of ownership it is lower and less aggravating than an outright purchase. Just keep in mind that this should not be an ongoing lifestyle choice as it is much more expensive than a straight purchase.

The "decision-maker" calculators normally found for buying a car are mainly for whether you get a lease vs. loan to acquire a car. In my view, this distinction is an irrelevant question over how much extra money you are going to throw away. I recommend that you do not throw any extra money away. My accurate calculator for buying any car is to select one of these:

1. Do you prefer to buy a car with cash?
2. Do you prefer to overpay by +25% by getting a car with a loan?
3. Do you prefer to overpay by +45% by getting a car through a lease?
4. Do you prefer to save 20-50% by purchasing a 2 to 3 year-old used car with low mileage for cash?

I prefer that you select option #4 unless you can afford option #1, but at least enter the transaction knowing how sharply you are affecting your financial life.

How much of your net worth is gone forever because you keep making some of these expensive choices for your cars? Go ahead and get the actual leasing numbers from a car dealer and include all of the fees and charges to get the car off of the lot. The extra charges tacked onto leases help make it the most expensive way to purchase the use of a car. By all means buy a car collection if you have the money and it makes you happy, but for most people, overpaying by 25–45% on every vehicle over a lifetime is a colossally-expensive mistake.

Also, don't forget to add an extra insurance cost whether you get a loan or a lease. When your down payment for a car is less than 20%, you will likely be required to further increase your cost with a gap insurance policy. If you are not forced to, it is a prudent decision because you are incurring the financial risk of being upside down (the car is worth less than the loan amount) in the event of an accident or early trade-in.

If you choose to ignore this advice about only paying cash for a car, make sure that you are not accidentally impairing your credit score. Many events can require an examination of your credit score including employment, a home mortgage, refinancing, or insurance. For example, mortgage lending guidelines generally require a car payment to be under 8% of your monthly gross income. If your loan or lease payment is above this number, then you either have to pay a higher rate or reduce the amount of the mortgage that you want. Like many qualifying numbers and ratios in banking, these numbers are derived from their experience. A car dealer once told me that one-third of the cars he sells with loans to people with low credit scores are repossessed for missed loan payments.

On the other extreme of repeat-car-leasers are the owners who drive a car until it is junked at a scrap yard for a nominal amount. If this is your transportation tactic, there are a few ideas you need to know. The average car taken to a junk yard for scrap is 15 years old and has about 225,000 miles. The quality of the car and your care help determine whether your particular vehicle will make it this far or well beyond this average. It is difficult to generalize about car repairs, but if a car has more than 150,000 miles, there is a risk that it could break down with an expensive repair. If your car has more than 150,000 miles, do you have the money saved for expensive maintenance costs (along with towing charges and car rentals), and enough to replace the vehicle if it is damaged beyond repair? Or will you have to borrow money and consume the savings you tried to build from driving an old car that also has cheap insurance? A car is an ongoing expense and you must continually save for a replacement and repairs while your car is working now.

Repair or replacement decision: as a car ages and loses value, it becomes more expensive to keep it in perfect condition. At a certain point in age and value, when you won't be getting much money if you were to sell the car, it may be too costly to repair minor functionality and aesthetic problems. You can then lower your insurance cost from comprehensive coverage to only liability coverage and start going to a local mechanic using refurbished parts instead of a high-priced dealership for maintenance. How long you choose to keep a car is your choice. As long as the car is reliable for you and maintenance expenses are not trending up, it can last +200,000 miles. Anytime the cost of a car repair is greater than the value of the car, you are better off selling the car as it is and replacing it with a car that doesn't need any repairs. My experienced mechanic says many people refuse normal maintenance or small repairs when they are cheap and wait until they snowball into catastrophic problems that cost 5-to-10 times what it would have cost to prevent these problems. At this point they face the dilemma of whether to junk the car and buy a new one when there would not have even been a problem if they had the reserves of money to properly maintain the car in a timely manner. (A commonly overlooked maintenance treatment he tells everyone, is to replace the coolant every few years; otherwise it eats the cooling system from the inside out).

Today, you can go online and chart out all of the costs of ownership over time: depreciation, insurance, maintenance, repairs, annual registration fees, etc. It is from these factors that an acquaintance taught me his "free car" method by focusing on how well a car maintains its value over time. He found a flat-spot on the depreciation curve for certain car models. In general, a car drops sharpest in value during its first few years and declines in value by a smaller amount in each successive year. For some models the value decline slows in years 2 through 5, and then begins another sharp drop beyond year 5 before expensive maintenance requirements start becoming due. My acquaintance bought a 3-year-old luxury car, drove it for 3 years, and then sold it for a small profit over the price that he paid for it. Sometimes the value flat-spots start as soon as 2 years but most of the time it is after 10 years. I have since read many variations of this tactic of isolating slow depreciation rates for certain car models to save money on your vehicles.

Debt Elimination Plan

If you have built up some personal debt there is no magic wand that can resolve it besides paying it off:

1. Get your credit reports and work to improve your credit score.
2. Call and negotiate with your lenders for lower interest rates than you currently have.
3. Transfer debt balances to the lowest rates that you can find.
4. Categorize your debts from the smallest personal debt to the largest personal debt.
5. Start making an extra principal payment to the smallest debt, making the minimum payments on all the remaining debts. By making the most extra principal payment to the smallest debt, it will be fully paid off the quickest, allowing you to allocate all the money that used be applied to this debt to the next largest. The psychological momentum of paying off a debt in its entirety and then moving on to extinguish the next one helps keep you motivated to stay on track. (Note that this method will extinguish your debts quickly unless there is a large disparity in the interest rates on your debt. If the difference between your highest interest rate and lowest interest rate is more than 5%, then you would be better off by prioritizing your personal debts instead from the highest interest rate to the lowest interest rate.)
6. Extinguish the debts one by one, and when one of them is paid off, use the full amount

you were paying toward the old debt to add to the extra principal payment of the next debt on your priority list.

There are too many caveats for the details of the ever-changing credit industry and your particular loans and credit—but do not move money to a new card or account until you verify a few items:

- The legitimacy of the company
- Pre-payment penalties
- Transfer fees
- Up-front interest charges
- Cash advance fees
- Annual account fees

As a simple rule to help avoid personal debts: if you do not want the item enough to save for it, then it probably will not be that rewarding for you to buy it with the extra expense of interest.

2. College/Trade Education

First, here are a few financial motivators for getting any advanced education: a college education can increase your lifetime earnings by $900,000[4], reduce your likelihood of being unemployed by over 54%[5], and is the best lever to move into the middle class or upper class income levels.

The typical teenager entering college normally does not have the financial acumen to understand when they are taking on more student loans than their career could ever repay. The worst case scenario is a new college student with no money who takes out student loans to pay for all tuition, room and board; year after year. Plus, they fail to get health insurance when they come down with an expensive illness. They end up with huge medical bills, huge student loans, and no degree because of illness or dropping out to get a full-time job to pay for immediate living expenses plus all the debt that they have acquired. In addition, student loans cannot be forgiven through bankruptcy; they will follow you and your credit rating until you extinguish them. Some financial awareness must be applied to determine the maximum amount that you should borrow for your education. For example, what is the average income that a graduate from your school earns with your major in the first 5 years? Is this enough income to pay down the outstanding loan balance that you will build up to get you through graduation? Do you have insurance to cover catastrophic risks like health, personal liability, automotive insurance, etc.? All of these expenses need to be considered thoroughly before you accept any college admissions offer where you will need loans to fund some of your education. Otherwise, the danger is that you will find yourself in some form of debt-nightmare where, even though you graduate and secure a job, student loans keep you financially crippled for decades. You may even need a second job just to earn enough to make the interest payments on all of the debt you that have piled up.

You should do the detail work of mapping out all of the expenses to determine how much money you will need to complete your degree. While you are doing this, here are the two inviolate rules about student loans:

First: Never borrow a penny during the first year of a four-year academic degree. One reason that you should never borrow money during the first year is because if you start out using loans as a funding source in your first year, then you will never be able to complete your degree without building up a catastrophic amount of debt. Borrowing money during the first year creates a predictable and unaffordable amount of student loans. A two or four year degree can accrue large expenses that will subsume your future income if you allow it. Do not start off with the bad habit of borrowing anytime you want money: if something is unaffordable, then borrowing money to buy it is a ticket for the debt-nightmare ride. Also, many people discover that going to a particular school or even getting any degree does not suit them. Switching to different majors, schools, trades, careers, travel, volunteering, or whatever is a very common occurrence for ages 17–24. However, if you have built up debt, it becomes an anchor that precludes you from moving on to other activities and careers that would be more suitable and fulfilling to you.

Second: Never exceed the 75% ratio of debt to your expected annual salary upon graduation (Total student debt divided by expected annual salary). This means that if you expect to earn a $35,000 salary in the first year of your chosen field from your school, then the maximum amount of money that you should allow yourself to borrow is $35,000 X 0.75, or $26,250. The remainder of your cost of schooling must be funded from sources that are not loans of any type. This 75% number should be surrounded with alarms and red lights because borrowing money beyond this ratio is financially catastrophic for your future. If you look up "student debt horror stories" you will find this 75% ratio violated every single time; in some cases it is exceeded many times over by unknowing students. Your expected salary is an unknown target, but it is relatively easy to estimate a range from your school's graduates with a similar degree. If you borrow beyond +75% of your expected salary, it can financially shackle every single area of your life for more than a decade. The loan payment will preclude you from moving out of your parents' home, buying a car, affording a wedding, having children, home ownership, starting a business, retirement planning, vacationing with friends, etc. If the interest rates on your student loans are unusually high, then the 75% ratio may even be too high as a threshold. Calculate if you can pay off all of your student loans within 5 years by spending 15% or less of your after-tax income. There are also exceptions to borrowing more than 75% (for example: degrees for professions with a high and expected increasing income such as dentistry, medicine, law, accounting, engineering, etc.). But in each case you must map out exactly how you can affordably pay down all of the debt in a short amount of time.

Beware that some professions require you to start in unpaid internships or start out new people on extremely-low journeyman incomes. If this includes your profession, then you cannot afford to have any student debt. You would not be the first graduate forced to take a higher-paying menial job (without advancement opportunity) simply to be able to start paying down the loans. This puts you in a position where you are not in a field that you trained for, may be forced to move back with your parents, and likely delay common financial milestones.

Funding sources for college include student loans, grants, scholarships, tax credits, work-study, employer assistance, many U.S. military programs, or financial aid from states/ federal agencies/community organizations. If more money is needed, choose a school with cheaper tuition, work part-time or full-time, and postpone entering school to save additional money. Some students attend cheaper community colleges for a year or two and then transfer to a state college to capture the best job recruiting opportunities. Determine which community college is the best "feeder school" for your state university and make sure every community-college class that you take will count as credit at the state school as well.

States offer financing programs that are normally called a Prepaid Tuition Program or Guaranteed College Tuition Program. These are contracts where you pay for tuition today when a student is at least 3 years away from entering college and in return you avoid the tuition increases during the intervening years. It can seem like a good deal to avoid the sharp increases in tuition and board when a child is younger, if you have the money. But I recommend that you avoid these types of programs. When tuition increases, these programs run deficits and change the rules for the people who have already enrolled. I cannot count the number of states that have altered their program rules to short-change participants in spite of using the word "guaranteed" in the program name. If tuition does not increase as expected, sometimes you would have been better off earning simple interest on the money that you put into the program. So whether tuition increases sharply or not, in my experience, parents come out financially behind by getting into these programs.

Another college savings vehicle is called a 529 Plan, which is a state-run account that offers tax advantages. Again, I do not recommend these programs due to high fees that go to the state, high commissions that go to the mutual fund companies, and poor investment returns from the mutual funds—along with the lack of investment options. Unlike most IRS qualified accounts, the 529 is run by individual states that use these accounts as assets to plunder:

- Upfront sales commissions can be over 5% of the amount invested
- Each state takes a percentage of assets that are held in these accounts

- Some states penalize out-of-state residents
- Some states tax accounts rolling from one 529 to another 529
- Some states assess tax penalties for changing 529 accounts
- There are states that offer up to 6 different plans to evaluate
- The 529 tax benefits were passed with "sunset laws" that may not be renewed
- Each state has different rules to evaluate

I think you get the point. There are other college savings vehicles (Coverdell ESA, Educational IRA, Educational Savings Bonds, etc.) but like all IRS-qualified accounts, they are subject to the whims of politicians and changing fortunes of the state and federal government. Even promoters of individual programs recommend that the risk of rule changes make putting all of your college money into a single type of account like these very imprudent. I can easily recommend that you do not put much money, if any, into any of these vehicles as the tax-efficiency does not offset the inflexibility, fees, poor investments, changing regulations; plus new programs become available every few years. There may be favorable rule changes by the time you read this, but read all of the fine print with great skepticism before you put any money into these plans.

A common dilemma is whether you should be saving for your children's college or your retirement. Ideally you would save for both, but that can be a difficult tradeoff on an average family income. The correct answer is: make sure that your savings rate is on track for your retirement first. Only when your retirement is on track can you then start to put aside money for their college costs. The reasoning behind this is that there are many sources of money for a college education but your personal savings is the primary source of your retirement fund. There is no retirement pot of gold that is magically waiting for you; even full social security benefits may not get you up to the poverty line. Your largest retirement source of money is drawn from what you have pre-paid into it plus what it may have grown into. Unlike prior generations, you can expect to be retired for 30 years and that is a lot of money that has to come from what you have built up for yourself. Your savings and your net worth are the only source for funding your retirement that you can consider with reliability.

It is best to save for college because parents who do not save any money for their children's college education pass on one of two legacies: either an inability to get a college degree (and all of the advancement opportunities that it provides), or a crippling amount of student debt. Before you get defensive that you paid for your degree all on your own prior to 1995, well, that was a very different time. Back then you could earn the money to cover college costs, but wages have stagnated for decades while college costs have soared. The ratio between entry-level job wages and tuition is nearly impossible for an average person at a medium-cost university. Parents (and the child) have 18 years to pile up at least 75% of the total cost of college; any more than that amount is a bonus toward minimizing what the student will have to earn or borrow to get his or her diploma.

3. Home Mortgage

Borrowing money to purchase a home is a unique personal expense. Financial advisers say "do not have debt, excluding your mortgage," but they do not explain why home debt is different than other debt. The explanation is that you must live somewhere, so you are going to have a housing expense no matter what your living situation may be. The affordability that applies to all of your consumption also applies to your housing. You can either pay rent for a place to live, or substitute your rent payment with a mortgage payment to own a place to live. This is why your mortgage, as a debt, is different than other consumer debt. Below are the key issues for you to understand around mortgages before you sign on the dotted line.

Mortgage in Retirement

According to Winning Concept #3, we must look to the end and work our way back. Housing is likely to be one of your largest single expenses throughout your life. One of the elements of a successful retirement is that you have arranged your finances so that you do not have to make rent or mortgage payments when you are retired. For many people, this factor alone determines whether or not they may ever be able to retire. To accomplish this, you either need to set aside money each month in a reserve fund to make your rent payments in retirement, or you need to have fully paid off the mortgage on your home.

No matter which living situation you choose, there are costs linked to that place that continue to rise over time; whether you are paying these directly as an owner or indirectly as a renter. For example, property taxes, insurance, utilities, appliances, and maintenance services generally rise over time. This makes home ownership more attractive in geographic areas where home prices are likely to rise during the time that you are planning to live there, or at a time when interest rates are low and susceptible to increasing.

Mortgage Amortization

An amortizing loan is created when part of the monthly payment pays the interest and an additional part pays down the principal loan balance. This is commonly referred to as equity buildup with a standard amortizing mortgage. Depending on the loan rate, the amount of the monthly payment that pays down the outstanding balance starts at under 15% and then slowly increases to 99% of the payment by the end of the term of the mortgage. Once your mortgage has been paid off, you are forever free from the three largest expenses of home ownership:

- The cost of the land.
- The cost of the building.
- The cost of the money to acquire the land and building.

If you ever get a mortgage, be sure that the term of the loan will end before any probable retirement date. You need your mortgage to amortize down to zero so that you will have no housing expense during your retirement. Or, be sure to have a careful plan mapping out how your mortgage will be affordable on your retirement income.

If it is your choice or circumstances to always rent, then the equity buildup of an amortizing mortgage is unavailable to aid in making your retirement more affordable. In this case, it is up to you to do it on your own by setting up a rental reserve. The amount of money to place into this reserve is 20% of your current rent payment. Anytime you make a rent payment, you should also be putting an additional 20% of that amount into this retirement rent fund. If there is a time when you want to own a home then this fund can be used for the down payment to purchase a home as well.

Home as an Investment

The concept of your home as an investment is an additional layer on top of "you must live somewhere and have a housing expense." The investing concept occurs because the market value of real estate changes and anytime there is a sale there will be a capital gain or loss on that sale. There are a many factors affecting your home's value, but most of them do not rapidly change. For example, a change in the quality of the school system, average income, the crime rate, new construction rate, etc. However, there are two predominant forces on your home's value: the increase or decrease of jobs in the local area, and the condition of your home. When there is an influx of jobs it puts upward pressure on home values and when jobs are leaving the area it puts downward pressure on home values. The condition of your home depends on what home buyers are looking for in your home's price range. This normally refers to how new your roof, furnace, carpet, or driveway may be. Also, if your home is not periodically updated then it may be less desirable and less valuable. For example, home features, materials, appliances, fixtures, colors, and amenities go in and out of style. If you want to maximize the investment value of your home, you need to be able to afford the repairs, maintenance, and upgrades necessary to keep your home desirable by the current market.

Home Buying Requirements

Just because a bank approves you for a mortgage to purchase a home does not mean that you can afford to own that home. There are four requirements that you need to be able to meet that will minimize the likelihood of your mortgage turning into a financial bear-trap.

First, if you have not saved a 20% down payment then you

are taking on more risk and expense. The expense is the extra cost of private mortgage insurance that will be required from the lender. The risk of a low down payment is that you do not have enough equity to survive the normal fluctuations in real estate values and you may lose what down payment you put into the home. If you need to relocate to another state but had only put 3% down, and then your home fell in value by 10% (plus you may have to pay a realtor to sell it for you), you may be better off financially by walking away from the home and letting it go into foreclosure. The more equity you have in any asset increases your financial options, flexibility, and stability.

The second requirement is a fixed-rate mortgage. Anytime that you have a mortgage with a variable rate, or one that must be refinanced in a certain number of years, you are pulling the pin on a financial grenade and hoping that you can get it back in before it blows you out of your home. For example, let's say you chose a mortgage that has an extra-low rate for three years and then in the fourth year it jumps up to the market interest rate plus 2 percent. You and the lender believe this isn't a problem, you'll just refinance before it jumps up into some other cheaper mortgage. In banking terms, you have just put yourself into a balance sheet mismatch; your loan was only for 3 years but you planned to live in the home much longer than that. What you have actually done is put all of your home equity at risk for several grenade pins:

- If you are unemployed or have a drop in income when you need to refinance, then you may be unable to get any loan.
- If your credit rating falls for some reason, you may be unable to get a loan or one at an affordable interest rate.
- If interest rates have gone up, there may be no mortgage interest rate available that is affordable for you.
- Mortgage guidelines change and your circumstances may no longer qualify for a reasonably-priced loan
- The value of homes in your area may have fallen and there isn't enough equity to refinance

All of these scenarios end with you being forced out of your home and possibly foreclosed upon. This was predictable from the start because you failed to get a fixed-rate, fully-amortizing loan. To pick up a few pennies with a cheaper mortgage payment, you gambled with your home equity, your credit rating, and with the possibility of being forced to move your family. You should interpret any variability or deadline in a mortgage as an unnecessary risk of default—never accept them.

The third requirement is mapping out the cost of ownership. Here are a few examples of the repair, replacement costs, or ongoing expenses that you may need to afford: exterior paint, interior paint, roof, driveway, furnace, air-conditioner, windows, trash removal, homeowners association, hot water heater, refrigerator, tree trimming, pest control, carpeting, etc. To maintain the livability and marketability of your home you may have to pay for all of these items. Complete a savings schedule that includes the cost and average lifespan to make a rough estimate of what you may need in a home maintenance fund. Every professional property manager makes an exhaustive list like this for rental properties to make certain the rent is high enough to cover the full cost of ownership of the rental unit.

The fourth requirement for purchasing a home is that you plan on being in the home at least 5 years. If you are not planning to be in a home that long then you are nearly guaranteeing a loss when you sell the home. The closing costs to purchase and then sell, including the realtor commission, the mortgage points, transfer taxes and fees, etc., make it nearly impossible to overcome with an increase in value or amortization in four years or less.

Refinancing Your Mortgage

The traditional decision-making method to determine whether or not to refinance is to calculate your monthly savings with the new lower payment and divide that into the cost of refinancing. This gives you a break-even point of how many months it will take to recover the closing costs. If you are planning to be in the home longer than this break-even date, then you would agree to do this refinancing. For example, if refinancing today would save you $200 per month and it cost $4,600 to close on this mortgage, then $4,600 divided by $200/month yields 23 months for you to recover this cost with your savings. If you plan to be in the home much longer than 23 months, then it would save you money beyond the break-even date so you would decide to take the loan.

Please do *not* use that decision-making method because it ignores a critical financial element: extending the payoff date of your mortgage. Always examine the entire cost of any transaction. If you have a 30-year mortgage and have paid it down for 12 years, then there are only 18 years remaining until the loan is gone. But if you refinance with another 30-year mortgage, then the 18-year payoff date is now extended back out to 30 years. This is a 67% increase in the term of the loan that you will be paying interest. To ignore lengthening the term of the mortgage is a huge decision-making mistake. So while you believe that you are saving money and becoming more financially stable, you have put yourself into a position to dramatically increase your interest costs that is actually consuming your income and reducing your financial stability.

In order to include the loan term in your calculations, get the potential new mortgage amortization schedule into a spreadsheet or online application. As an adjustment, take the monthly savings and add all of it as an extra principal payment each month. Then check and see if the mortgage would be paid off sooner or later than the old mortgage. If the monthly savings is not enough to pay down the loan as fast as the old mortgage, then the new mortgage you are examining would leave you financially worse off if you refinanced with it. If the monthly savings does extinguish your mortgage faster than the old one, then it is financially favorable for you to take this mortgage—if you are disciplined enough not to spend the monthly savings but to apply it to the mortgage balance every month.

Additional Principal Payments

Obviously, it is more financially favorable for you to build up equity faster rather than slower. If you can afford a mortgage with a term of less than 30 years (25, 20, or 15), then you can access even lower mortgage rates that will accelerate your equity build-up even faster. But a 30-year mortgage gives you the most flexibility on when to make extra principal payments, rather than be forced to make them as you would with a shorter-term mortgage. By simply making one extra mortgage payment each year you can take many years off the term of a mortgage of any length.

Whether you have mortgage equity build-up or a rental reserve that you've funded, 70% of the net worth of retirees is in their home.[6] If you do not manage your finances to build this up, you will miss out on an important aspect of your future financial stability.

Borrowing Money for Home Improvements

Home maintenance and repairs are a normal and expected part of your housing cost, and they are a personal expense. Like all personal expenses, you should never purchase them with borrowed money. If you have mapped out the cost of ownership as recommended, you should already have the money set aside for any maintenance, repairs, or upgrades that may be needed. If you have not done this or set aside the money, then you were living above your means and it is time to either reduce your spending or move somewhere cheaper where you can afford normal maintenance and repairs.

There are two exceptions for borrowing money for home repairs or improvement. First, if there is a problem that makes the home unlivable that you need to address (and you have mapped out paying down this loan and it is affordable), then it is unfortunate but necessary. The second exception is if changes in your circumstances (more children, adult parents moving in, etc.) require an addition or improvement that will allow you to stay in the home rather than move. Of course, all of this must meet your guidelines for affordability, but in this case, it is acceptable to borrow money to make this happen.

If you are trying to sell your home, most home improvements will not be fully reflected, dollar-for-dollar, in the sale price. These are normally a net investment loss and should never be done on borrowed money unless they are needed to make the home marketable at all and the debts are easily affordable to you if the home does not sell.

4. Income-Producing Investments

Borrowing money to purchase an investment that produces predictable income offers the potential to create a favorably-leveraged profit. It is the primary operation of a bank: to borrow money at a lower rate and lend it out at a higher rate, making a profit on the difference. This profit mechanism is called favorable leverage: the rates that you earn are greater than the rates that you owe. Similar to banking operations—you also need to have many, many safeguards in place to keep from imploding from either side—a mismanaged loan or a poor performing investment—and the cash flow timing between the two.

Putting your money into *any* investment with borrowed money requires professional-level experience and full-time, up-to-date knowledge. If you are borrowing money to invest, it is even more important for the investment to be diligently managed by you to ensure its success. As with every debt, its repayment must be affordable to your income if the investment fails from the first day or performs poorly over time. I highly recommend that the amount of money that you borrow can be fully paid back within two years. If it takes more than two years to pay it all back, then you are risking far too much money and destroying too much of your net worth from a loss on a single investment.

Beware that interest on personal debts is not tax deductible, in general. Your investments may need to be held in some type of legal entity where this is permitted. Some people mismatch their leverage: they expect to use pre-tax returns to make post-tax deduction interest payments. Map out your investment cash flow with expert guidance so you avoid the common investor mistakes.

5. Investments Solely for Capital Gains

Borrowing money for an investment seeking capital gains is a very risky game only for very experienced players with a lot of knowledge. I am not against doing this, however, I want to dissuade anyone who would consider doing this without professional expertise and very prudent management. The most vivid example of the dangers of this type of debt that I can remember is about a Japanese company. It was a family-held company going back 38 generations that built temples for over 1,400 years.[7] This fabled-construction company went bankrupt in 2006 because they borrowed money to speculate in real estate that they hoped to develop for a large profit. They made the classic mistake: they borrowed more money than they could afford to pay back and bought property at the top of a real estate bubble just before prices collapsed. This company borrowed even more money in order to make debt payments until they could no longer do so. This rare business legacy was then liquidated to a competitor.

It is very dangerous to borrow for capital gains! You need a lot of knowledge, a lot of experience, and a lot of cash reserves. Debt does not allow for patience because it has an expiration date and the payments are not extinguished until all the principal is paid back with interest. Like all debt, the amount must be affordable to your income and you should easily be able to pay it back even if the investment fails within two years. Earning money solely from capital gains is a gamble. Like all gambles, you need to afford several attempts (gambles or speculations) to make sure you give yourself the possibility that one might be successful enough to cover the losses on the unsuccessful ones. It is my recommendation that if you borrow money to make an investment, that the principal amount of all of these combined make up less than 10% of your investment portfolio. Prudent risk management must be more important than reaching too far and experiencing a catastrophic loss to your net worth or imperilling your assets.

Winning Concept #7

Decisions involving a commitment of either value or time always create opportunity costs. It is your fiduciary duty to discover and minimize as many of these costs as possible before you unknowingly incur them.

The confusing concept of an opportunity cost is defined as the price of not doing something else. When you choose to engage in an activity, you are simultaneously excluding other activities during that same time period. Those activities that you excluded are opportunities to you that are lost forever during that same time period. It is these excluded activities that economists label as an opportunity cost. The definition of opportunity costs that is focused on in this book may be easier to understand: missing money; all of the money that is missing from your wallet if you had acted more prudently. If you had acted with more financial awareness and diligence, then there would be minimal opportunity costs because you were able to capture that money for your wallet. These opportunity costs will likely be in the form of estimates and probabilities, but the process of thinking through scenarios will force you to make much better financial decisions.

Let's start with a simple example: you have $1,000 in a savings account at a bank earning 1% interest for a year, or $10. A bank across the street was offering 5% during the same period for a potential $50 in interest income. You could have earned $50 across the street but, since you did not, it cost you $40 ($50 minus $10) in opportunity costs. The extra $40 that could have been in your wallet is not there because you did not take advantage of the higher interest rate during that time period. Similarly, all actions and inactions have opportunity costs attached to them.

In another example, if you spend an hour teaching yourself how to juggle with several tennis balls, it seems like an activity that was free. This is not true in economics, the opportunity cost of that hour spent juggling is determined by everything else that you could have been doing during that hour (cooking dinner, coming up with a medical cure, or adding to the conversation with some neighbors). Among all of the activities that you could have been doing instead of juggling, the largest opportunity cost would likely be if you had used that time to earn an extra hour of wages. If you could have earned $10 in that hour, the opportunity cost of your hour of juggling cost was $10. This is only one potential opportunity cost (not every hour of the day could be spent working). It is also possible that you were learning a valuable skill that could earn you money by performance entertainment. Another opportunity cost would have been if you were juggling to procrastinate and avoid an appointment for a job interview. In this case, the cost of your juggling is the earnings from the job that you do not have because you excluded that possibility from occurring during the same period of time. The study of financial opportunity costs is the discovery and evaluation of the most accurate estimates of what you are excluding from happening. These are decisions where you are financially worse off because you made a choice that was less than optimal.

Everyone already has their own intuitive way of doing this to a degree, showing you a few specific examples will help reveal how to put the idea of opportunity cost into practical application for yourself. I only want to expose the basic definition without the economic vocabulary or mathematics in order to focus on practical applications that directly affect your finances.

Again, an opportunity cost is the gap between where you are financially and where you could have been better-off financially if you had made a different choice. As an example, let's say that you are meeting someone today to sell your car. The car needs a repair that you meant to complete yesterday, but it was such a nice day that you went fishing instead. The buyer shows up today but because of the uncompleted repair, he lowers the price of what he will pay by $500. In the world of money, one of the prices that you just paid for your day of fishing is $500 in cash on the sale of your car. But this expense is not real, it is an opportunity cost. The $500 that could have been in your wallet is not there, and nobody can see that it is missing (except people who are financially literate). To economists, you just took $500 out of your wallet and threw it into the fishing pond. In the world of economics, that day of fishing may have been more satisfying to you than the $500 in cash that you lost on the car sale; making it a rational and satisfying decision.

My reason for highlighting opportunity costs at all is this: wouldn't you prefer to know how much your day of fishing was going to cost you before you took it, so that you could have decided with the most knowledge to attain your best outcome, financial or otherwise? As you earn more money, accumulate more, and control more valuable assets, these opportunity costs become larger and more complex. Would your feeling about losing the $500 for the car repair change if instead the fishing trip had cost you $50,000 on the sale of your house? Or it cost you a career change that would have benefited you by an extra $100,000 over the next 10 years? Or it cost you a business partnership that could have earned you $250,000?

When you understand opportunity costs, then you have more financial options. Had you been skilled with opportunity costs when selling that car, you could have captured more of that extra $500. If the $500 were not important, you could have made that decision and been free from any stress of thinking about the repair while you were fishing. If the $500 were important to you, then you could have worked at night to complete the repairs. Or, you could have hired someone to do it for you at a price less than $500, and still come out ahead. If you were not thinking about opportunity cost with good estimates, you might have paid $750 for the repair from which you gained only $500, unknowingly resulting in a realized loss of $250 in cash.

Concept #7 refers to considering all of the significant opportunity costs that you are incurring from your life decisions. Financial stability is increased by capturing financial opportunities and minimizing both real and opportunity costs.

It is possible to incur an opportunity cost by not being aware of market seasons (selling a boat in the snowy winter), market cycles (buying real estate as employment in the area is still falling sharply), the depreciation of time, or the devaluation from obsolescence (you procrastinated on selling your car or electronics and now you are trying to sell it just after a new and improved model was released).

A common opportunity cost that many people are unaware of is accumulated costs. For example, let's say that you inherited a very valuable painting worth $100,000 that you want to sell.

Since the painting appraised at $100,000, that is its value and you won't accept anything less than that amount. You receive an offer of $95,000 for this painting and the buyer will not pay any more than this amount. But you do not want to be ripped-off with a low offer—so you decide to reject this buyer's offer and wait for another buyer to get your full value of $100,000. While you are waiting, there are opportunity costs that are conceptually ratcheting up around you. For example, if you had accepted the offer of $95,000 and were able to invest that money at 5% then you could have been earning $395 per month in interest income. This is an opportunity cost of rejecting the $95,000 offer. Add to this the insurance cost of $50 per month and a temperature/humidity controlled storage unit for the painting of $75 per month. These three costs add up to $520 per month. The insurance and storage are real costs you are paying out-of-pocket, but the largest expense is the $395 of opportunity cost in the form of lost-interest income that is missing from your wallet. You have rejected an offer of $95,000 in order to potentially get an extra $5,000. How long can you wait? The answer is calculated by dividing the marginal gain by the amount of the cost for waiting, or $5,000 gain divided by $520 cost per month = 9 months. In only 9 months, your expenses will have consumed the entire $5,000 gain that you were waiting for. Do you think that it is important for your decision-making to know this exact date? Yes, of course, because each month after the 9th month that you have not sold the painting, you have lost another $520 that you will not recoup even if you receive the full price of $100,000. After the 9th month, you have to raise your selling price by $520 each month in order to break-even; to be at the same place that you would have been financially had you initially sold it at the first offer of $95,000. Every month you are throwing $520 into the wind until you sell that painting. Most people make the mistake of focusing on the extra $5,000 opportunity and ignore all of the accumulating costs and tasks associated with capturing that extra money, and inadvertently end up with far less money than they could have had. I cannot count the number of people I know who wanted to get rid of an item—but their lack of awareness resulted in many inadvertent opportunity costs. In the worst case; I have even seen many gifts and inheritances ultimately leaving the recipients financially worse off than if they had received nothing.

There are accumulated costs of ownership for every asset that you control, in both real and opportunity costs. The real costs are your cash outlays and the opportunity costs are all the monies that are missing from your wallet because you failed to act with more financial awareness. When you no longer want a valuable object, there are two target prices that you want to compare:

1. Your maximum opportunity (time needed for a full price offer to arrive, condition of object is fully refurbished, item is moved to location of highest demand, marketing exposure to the most number of interested buyers)
2. Your minimum opportunity (time = today, condition = as it is right now, location = current place, marketing exposure limited to quick and cheap or free)

Both of these prices are moving targets that change over time. But the cost of ownership, in addition to the cost repairing , moving, and marketing the item from the minimum to the maximum target price, only ratchets in one direction, and that is higher until the sale is completed. In addition to these costs, the opportunity cost for you to calculate is the amount of money that it would be earning for you if you sold it at your minimum target price today. Next, calculate a break-even point where the accumulated real and opportunity costs rise to above your maximum target price. In the prior example with the painting, you could have estimated: do I have the time, marketing expertise, and access to enough art buyers to get the full $100,000? Can I hire experts to accomplish all of these tasks and still have money left over after paying all of them?

Opportunity costs also arise in the form of any obstacle to the disposition of a valuable asset. A project management schedule of tasks that need to be performed will reveal your optimal list of actions to take (the order that they need to be performed and the dates by which they need to be performed). Any delay of the critical deadlines builds up both real costs and opportunity costs. Whatever you are doing instead of the critical tasks is exactly how you are shredding your money in additional costs. You may also be shredding your money by avoiding hiring and managing the people who could be getting critical tasks completed for you. For example, if you are watching TV instead of getting a valuable task completed, imagine a money-meter on top clicking away as long as the TV is on; if you are helping a neighbor, imagine taking money out of your wallet and stapling it to the side of their house; if you are working on any non-critical task for your project, imagine that to continue this task is exactly like putting money into a slot machine with no possibility of a payout: you keep putting money in but nothing can come out.

Let's talk about repairing things by yourself to get them ready for sale; home, car, clothing, electronics, etc. When it comes to completing tasks that you may know how to do on your own, a common error is I-Can-Do-It-Myself Syndrome. This is where you do not hire an efficient professional and instead muck around and burn money in opportunity costs because:

1. You believe that you have all of the necessary skills and knowledge to complete a task; but you do not, and make mistakes that end up adding more in costs and delays.
2. You have the skills and knowledge to complete a task, but you are so much slower than a professional that the delays end up costing more than hiring someone to complete the task.
3. You have the skills and knowledge to complete a task, so you cannot bring yourself to pay someone else, but you do not have the time to complete it within any reasonable time-frame.
4. You are effectively completing a small part of the project, but in the meantime, other aspects of the project are delayed because no one is managing other important aspects of the entire project.

The largest opportunity cost that many people pay is the loss of net worth due to low or no savings on a continual basis.

Financial planners are justified in their exuberance over the benefit of compound interest. Here are the basics: Over your working career, putting a $1 bill into a piggy bank every day would physically pile up into over $16,000. If that money were accumulating in an interest-earning account, it could accrue into $30,000 (with a rate of 2.5%). In the hands of a diligent investor it could launch above $158,000 (at a rate of 8%), possibly above $315,000 (at a rate of 10%). This is just with $1 per day; the results become correspondingly larger when you chart them with what you are likely to be earning and could potentially set aside. Would you consider starting on a plan of saving $1/day–*or more*? Consistent savings is the most realistic, easy, and stable manner in which to build your net worth and will be the biggest difference between the lifestyle that you have and a much wealthier one that you could have had.

Other common opportunity costs:

1. Education: not getting certifications or degrees, avoiding advanced training.
2. Knowledge: not keeping up to date with your profession or personal finance issues.
3. Career: staying home to raise children and not receive the income, pay raises, benefits, retirement contributions and perks that you could have earned over a career. Although most of the factors for this decision are non-financial, many parents only give a cursory guess at the financial effect of the month-to-month cash flow for the household. Staying home with children sharply truncates your lifetime earnings. Even if you return to work, the pay rate will be lower and your lifetime earnings will be significantly smaller, your peak earnings will be at a much lower rate, and your retirement/pension accounts will be smaller. If you are planning for a spouse to quit a job to raise children, go ahead and see for yourself if you can actually afford to do it by not spending their income for a year. This will highlight whether your family can survive on one income and give you a financial buffer when you start.

Winning Concept #8

You must play financial offense if you desire financial success. Playing financial defense by managing your expenses is important, but it is more critical to employ an offensive plan to continually earn an increasing amount of money.

Your financial success depends on playing both offense and defense. Many articles and books on money discuss defensive tactics such as reducing your expenses by making your own laundry detergent, extreme couponing, drive an old car until it falls apart, and meticulously budget your money. If your spending is out-of-control beyond your income, of course it is paramount that you examine your spending to sharply reduce your expenses. However, even if you are moderately aware of all of your spending, there is little benefit to focus on reducing these expenses further. Yes, you need to spend a little time each year to see if you can get a better price on your major expenses, but this should *not* be your main activity for financial gains.

For example, let's say that you were given an assistant with 100 hours of time that was already paid up. You could only give him or her one of two tasks: reducing your expenses or increasing your income. Which one would provide you the greater benefit? If you are reasonably aware of your expenses and manage them, it is unlikely that your assistant would be able to discover anything but tiny incremental savings. However, if you used your assistant to market your services toward something that you enjoy doing, it could lead to a new ongoing income stream for your finances.

I recommend that you always be executing an offensive plan to increase your earned income. If you fail to do this, then sooner than you expect, your income will plateau and your dreams and goals may be left starved for funding that you cannot provide them. So what has been your offensive plan up to this point? I want to provide you with some general guidelines to help in this important effort.

For Employees:

Here are 6 time-tested strategies to consider for maximizing your earnings during your career:

1. If you are earning a low or minimum wage this is a signal that you are not providing the workplace much value. Increase your financial capability immediately by getting training, certifications, an apprenticeship, acquiring a mentor, or the experiences that are required to move into ever-higher paying positions. Securing and then maintaining a very high paying job is never an accident that you will stumble upon. Putting yourself on track for these positions starts with the best entry-level position you can get. Naturally, these jobs are much easier to obtain with diplomas, credentials, internships, extra coursework, additional certifications, favorable work history of promotions, etc. Do you belong to your professional association so that you can network and discover opportunities? Are you getting all the certifications that are available to increase your value? Are you absolutely certain there is nothing else you can do to be viewed as more valuable to an employer vs. other employees?

2. As a general rule, the more people and money that you are in charge of, the more income you can demand. To start off, as fast as possible look to get into a position that includes supervising other people. After you become a supervisor, look for a position that also includes responsibility for a company budget. As you achieve positions with ever-larger supervisory and budget responsibilities, you want to be looking for a position that includes the revenue side as well, full P&L responsibility (profit and loss statement). Once you have P&L responsibility you are targeting ever greater divisions/groups/companies with larger P&L numbers. This is the general path for the highest salary and bonus increases—more people to supervise along with increasing financial responsibilities.

3. Whatever company you are in, the highest paid people will be working in the primary area of expertise of the business. All other departments in the company will have a lower salary range and budget. Supporting departments will also have less opportunity for advancement and development. For example, an engineering consulting firm will offer the highest salaries to the people adding the most value, i.e., the engineers with the most skill and experience. Other departments will be smaller with more limited opportunity and certainly less salary; such as human resources, accounting, administrative support, technical or computer support, etc. Using this logic, if your background is in human resources, then the best opportunities for you will be in a company specializing in providing human resource consulting or services. In any other type of company, your department is an expense to be minimized which limits your future opportunity and income. So the critical question is—are you currently working in the primary area of expertise for your company? If not, start looking for jobs in companies where your specialty is the primary expertise of the company as well.

An exception to this "business expertise" track is sales positions. A sales position that has a commission component can earn a very high income compared to the rest of the company payroll. In sales, the larger the transaction size, the larger the potential commission income—so reach for higher priced items until you find an area where your aptitude is best suited (TVs, cars, homes, commercial loans, business software systems, apartment complexes, private businesses, public businesses, etc.).

4. If you are a sole contributor (such as a mechanic, appraiser, dentist, scientist, carpenter), the path of increasing earnings is built upon increasing expertise and experience. Expertise comes from training, this can either be on-the-job, academic, or from additional certifications. In the beginning of your career, you should be seeking ever-diverse projects and cases but also ever-more complicated and difficult projects. As you discover a specialty for yourself that is paid the most, or has the brightest future, then you should seek the most depth in this area and avoid further diversification. Your experience and expertise will still increase the more you seek complicated and difficult assignments in this area and succeed with them. At this point, your work that is compensated the most will fall in this area and your pay will drop to a lower market price whenever you are working on projects only requiring general skills.

5. No matter which profession you choose, the best opportunities for income are provided by growth from the fastest-growing: company, industry, region, or country. The more growth in revenue that a company has, the more opportunity there will be for rapid advancement, responsibility, and skill development that becomes yours to take to any other career opportunity. Successful, growing, or profitable businesses also have the most money available for management training, classes, equipment and software, and courses to expand your skill set and marketability. Industry-leading companies that are growing and profitable also provide better raises, benefits, bonuses, and perks. I also mentioned geographic region because growing areas, cities, and countries can quickly offer you opportunities that might take a decade in more mature areas. Are you living in a high-growth area for your expertise?

6. Some of you may prefer stability over a flashy new company that may be all the rage one year, and fade the moment something new comes along next year. In this case you need to find a mature industry—but only choose one of the industry leaders within this group. The older the company and more mature the industry, the more likely you will have a stable career with the company. Alone, this is not a financially offensive tactic; however, the increased stability from this type of career choice may permit you to take more risk with side projects and investments that you might not ordinarily take.

Some people may now complain, "Money isn't everything in a job," "What if I don't like the job?" "Those jobs take away too much time from my family." The answer to these is simple—these strategies for higher earnings simply work. It is up to you to fit them into your personal career, if at all. These are the time-tested tactics for you to maximize your career's income potential. Now you are aware of them so you will avoid complaining 20 years from now, "Why didn't anyone tell me I was stunting my income and career so severely!" The point is to help you find higher paying areas as long as they fit within your personality and capability. No matter which career you select there are two certainties: 1) A predictable salary arc that you will experience based upon your career choice. 2) A day in your future when your salary will plateau and then fall. This section was written to help you increase your salary arc and to delay that date of plateau and decline for as long as possible.

Many people have no interest to run up the corporate ladder. This is a good thing and can be additional motivation to set aside more of your pay for: training in a career that you would better enjoy, transition to something more meaningful and satisfying, or fund your own business in order to run it the way you believe it should be run. If nothing else, that money will be set aside to ramp up your other financial offensive strategies.

Other Offensive Strategies

No matter what your day job is, it is only the beginning base of your potential earnings. There are two primary ways to begin your financial offense:

1. Side Service Business: Anyone 16-years or older has many skills that they can sell locally. For example there are many tasks that you likely already know how to do, such as: dog walking, house/pet sitting, lawn service, cleaning service, tutoring, window washing, assisting the elderly, running errands, organizing, etc. You get the idea. For the cost of a flyer or internet ad and a few supplies, you can be in business earning money within a few days. There are also many websites offering freelance work where you can earn money from home on your computer.

Other services may require some training: computer support, advanced tutoring, building websites, music lessons, etc. but nearly everyone can move toward providing a higher-skill service that commands more money.

2. Tangible Investing: Buying a physical object below its market value and selling it at a higher price somewhere else. For example, buying a book at a garage sale for $1 and selling it online for $10. Now, $9 is not a lot of money, but I know someone who has automated so much of this that he makes a meaningful annual income solely from flipping used books from garage sales.

Another example: I bought unused TV satellite dishes for $20 and sold them to a distributor in Puerto Rico for $65.

He would buy all that I could provide to him. I posted an ad and went around making offers on these dishes. The money that I made from these satellite dishes over a summer became 25% of the down payment that I made on a rental home. I was trading up into yet another tangible investment, one that has been providing tax-sheltered income for years. Naturally, none of this income is spent, it is directed toward other net worth building.

If you want to advance further, combine your service together with tangible investing. Here are a couple business models:

- Buy an X in bad condition, fix it up, and then resell it in significantly better condition. Where X can be most anything = furniture, lamps, computers, cellphones, copiers, coke machines, motorcycles, clothing, cars, homes, boats, commercial real estate, businesses, etc. Just about anything where you have an interest is likely to have some component that you could transform into an income producer.

- While providing your service you can also add on physical products. For example, while you are offering a dog walking service, you can buy dog food in bulk and deliver it to your customers. While you provide a computer troubleshooting service, you could also sell them customized computers/components at a markup.

If you do not have some service or investing business, then your income is solely dependent on the vagaries of your local labor market and supervisor. To me, this is wasting your personal potential, incurring a huge opportunity cost of lost income and investment compounding growth. Plus, in my opinion, it is foolishly reckless to put your financial life solely in someone else's hands—someone who has no vested interest in your personal or financial success.

Empire Building

Would you prefer to have several employers bidding against each other to hire you? Outside of professional sports and celebrity entertainers, do you hear of this happening? Well, you are about to learn how to get into that position, starting with no education or experience, plus make money as an investor.

For the average person to position themselves for a career in high demand, you must become a profitable operator. An operator is someone who understands a small business operation from A to Z, and can manage it in a profitable manner. Here are some examples of operations that are small enough and simple enough that nearly anyone can master: a laundromat, fast-food restaurant, self-storage facility, car wash, dry cleaners, property manager, pizza shop, oil change shop, vending machine route, etc.

Each of these businesses are self-contained units where you can get a part-time job starting at the bottom, and within a relatively short amount of time, work toward learning the entire business inside and out. Most people with this knowledge remain an employee and a few have the drive to become an owner of a single location. However, if you have enough financial ambition, this skill set can launch an empire.

Once you have reached a level of competency and are working toward mastery of the skills of your chosen business model, you want to raise money to buy your own business operation to manage. Whether you start out with an ownership stake of 50% or only 5%, you will be a business owner with cash flow from operations flowing into your checking account plus your salary.

Once you have completed one purchase and the business has stabilized under your management, it is time for you to train your replacement for that operation and then raise money again for your purchase of a second operation. Although your old salary will mostly go to your replacement, you still have the ownership income from that first business. When you purchase a second business, you now have a successful track record and, likely, a little of your own capital to invest so that you'll have even more ownership of the second operation. You repeat this cycle of "purchase, takeover, and stabilize" over and over again.

From here, you can expand into several directions. First, you can continue to expand shop by shop. Second, you can buy distressed business operations cheaply, take them over, turn them around and sell them for a profit. Third, you can change your cycle from doing individual business units to portfolios of these businesses. Here is a specific example: I was first exposed to this empire-building strategy when I became acquainted with someone who did this with Pizza Hut restaurants. He first learned to successfully manage a Pizza Hut, and then learned how to start them from scratch. He continued increasing his skills until he (along with a group of investors), bought territories from Pizza Hut. The group would do research to find good locations, build the buildings, hire and train the staff, and get them operating profitably until the entire territory was full of restaurants. He and his investors would then sell the entire territory of successfully operating restaurants back to Pizza Hut for a tremendous amount of money. It all started with some simple skills - do you think you could get a job at a fast-food restaurant, a car wash, or a real estate management company?

Once you prove that you are a profitable operator and part owner, local investors with money will start to seek you out. This will happen because investors and money managers are always seeking new investments with proven operators. You will receive phone calls from people you have never heard of, people who ignored you in the past will now want to become acquainted with you, and investor groups and bankers will wine-and-dine you to get your secrets or try to be the first in line to invest in your next project. People who want to sell their business operation will be calling you first. At this point you have passed the threshold where your reputation will be attracting opportunities instead of you having to seek them out. Not only have I seen this happen to others first-hand, it happened to me while I was in a foreign country to start a project. I arrived alone in Europe as an unknown person from a new company, and after a few weeks, I had established a successful reputation and deals started to chase me instead of the other way around. For example, I received an unsolicited call and found myself in a day-long meeting with a general manager. He and his staff were trying to convince me to hire his manufacturing team with orders in hand from a well-known German car company. Next, my law firm's managing partner took me out to an expensive lunch and wanted to hand me a Spanish clothing company looking to expand in Asia. I received another unsolicited call from a Polish manufacturer whom I had never heard of that wanted to invest in my current project. I mention these to highlight that anyone can do this anywhere. This strategy has been successful for many people in many industries who started without degrees, connections, mentors, or money. The biggest hurdle for the average person is to raise the money for your first transaction. Raising money is just another skill you can learn and then you will have some legal expenses to set it all up correctly. One way to make it easier for you is to initially seek employment at a business with an owner who already has multiple locations or multiple businesses. If you perform well, this owner may be predisposed to fund and assist in your first solo transaction.

This career strategy also ties into investing. You may want to invest with other people who are successfully employing this exact strategy. You want to invest with them into projects before they get too big and successful and no longer need any investors. What commonly happens is they do so well for their early investors that they become very sought after. At this point they either start increasing minimum investment levels to something well beyond your capability or they only offer average returns to investors and keep the bulk of the profit for themselves.

Winning Concept #9

Taxes (of all kinds) are your largest expense so reducing them is imperative to increase your earnings and net worth. Taxes apply to every transaction and your goal is to legally drive your tax liability as low as possible.

There is no such thing as earning or profiting "before-taxes" because the tax rules always apply. As a U.S. citizen, each transaction that you make is subject to tax laws and they apply worldwide. Knowing how to reduce and eliminate any kind of tax with your spending and investing will have an enduring impact on your financial success.

Tax laws are written to favor or hinder various activities. If you act in alignment with the goals of governing authorities and their current favored activities, then you will be rewarded with tax benefits. Otherwise, you are obligated to pay normal tax rates or possibly punitive tax rates. These tax policies change every year but the principles will remain the same.

The Three Tax Levers

There are 3 levers that you can manipulate to your advantage in reducing your tax liabilities:

1. First Lever: Source of income. Your income, for tax purposes, is all placed among three different categories:

a) Wages earned from a job are subject to the highest income tax rates. The tax code calls this the "ordinary income tax rate". This ordinary income tax rate also applies to consulting or other jobs and business where your pay is a rate based upon your time. Since ordinary income is taxed at the highest rates, reducing this type of income provides the greatest opportunity to keep more of your money.

b) Profit earned from investments is called portfolio

income. This includes capital gains and dividends. The tax rate on portfolio income is more complicated to compute, but if you hold an investment for a certain period of time you are subject to a more favorable long-term capital-gains tax rate.

c) The third type of income is called passive income by the IRS. This includes income from a business in which you do not materially participate. There are many specific rules to determine what is and what is not passive income but the two most common types are business partnerships or rental property where you are not involved in the operations. The benefit of passive investments is that deductions from the business can reduce your personal taxes, within some limitations. For example, people who qualify as a professional real estate investor, according to IRS rules, can often reduce their tax liability to zero on real estate income. Every country offers favorable tax incentives for passive income investors in order to accomplish a goal. These political goals can include economic development in an area hit with a devastating storm, a particular business that offers jobs or housing, or a strategic industry that the politicians want to develop. (Tax credits are even available for owning a race horse or vineyard in some states).

2. Second Lever: Where you choose your residency and where you spend your money. Where you choose to live can have a dramatic impact; the difference of just a few miles can possibly provide you favorable treatment on property taxes, sales tax, city income tax, and others.

Planning where and how you spend your money can also reduce your tax liability. Aside from the location of making purchases in a low-sales tax area, certain items can have reduced or no sales tax. For example, some states allow used cars, clothing, mobile homes, or boats to be purchase without sales tax.

3. Third Lever: Investment location and the type of investment. The location of an investment refers to the entity holding the investment. Is it in a partnership that is held in a trust or just your own name? Is it in a tax-deferred IRA or held jointly with your spouse? The location of any investment will affect the tax treatment and likely the type of investment that would be best to hold in that location. As a simple example, a bond is a type of investment which produces interest income that is taxed at high-ordinary income-tax rates. Because of this, it is financially beneficial to hold bonds in tax-deferred accounts. Investments for capital gains can be held in your name because they are subject to lower capital-gains tax rates.

When evaluating investments, some sales people will want you to focus on a gross return, but you can't make a decision until you also subtract out the taxes for their strategy to your particular situation. The after-tax return to your circumstances is the only true measure that you can use to make any financial comparisons and decisions.

For another example, are these IRS qualified accounts a good investment: IRA, Roth IRA, 401(k), 403(b), SIMPLE, etc.? The answer is: they are just accounts with specific rules and a location-filter through which to evaluate the best place to hold your money. I have performed many evaluations for employees who have 401(k) accounts with employers who also provide a matching contribution. The majority of the time, calculations reveal that their particular 401(k) fees and investment options are so poor that they would have more after-tax income throughout their retirement years if they stopped their 401(k) contributions, withdrew all the money early, paid the 10% tax penalty, and invested it on his or her own. (Part of this is because the average two-worker family pays an average of $154,800 in hidden 401(k) fees that consume 35% of your investment returns.[8]) Non-intuitive solutions like this are only revealed when your entire lifetime of returns and taxes are analyzed. Have you done this with your own retirement plans to make certain you are maximizing your after-tax lifetime income?

One last tax to highlight is a hidden tax that everyone pays through higher prices that is more commonly called inflation.

Inflation is defined as a trend of increasing prices or the fall in value of a currency. For consumers that means any loss of purchasing power from your money. For example, if the cost of healthcare or tuition is higher than last year then you are being taxed by inflation. Since the U.S. Federal Reserve was founded in 1913, the U.S. dollar has lost 98.8% of its value compared to gold.[9] All paper currencies that are not backed by anything eventually devalue close to worthlessness. In well-managed economies this occurs slowly over decades and in the most poorly managed economies this occurs repeatedly every few years. Inflation is partially created by central bankers expanding the money supply because they prefer any inflation over deflation (falling prices). The other driver for inflation is called currency devaluation. This is an official lowering of the currency exchange rate to keep the economy operating; normally when politicians spend more than the country can borrow or payback. The effect of inflation or currency devaluation is that your money is subject to an ongoing drop in value. Is inflation a big deal when it is mostly between 1–3%? Let's say that you are retiring today with a fixed-income pension. Many retirees live 30 years after retirement, so 30 years times 2% is a total of 60% inflation, but with compounding it is actually 81% inflation. This number means that the value of your money will have dropped by 81% through the mechanism of a "low" inflation-rate of 2% over 30 years. Inflation is just an economic concept right up until the point that you are at the grocery store and cannot afford an 81% increase in prices on your fixed income. So this is a big financial landmine: you thought you were retiring early with a nice income but forgot to take into consideration the accumulation of inflation over a few decades. To maintain your spending level it is imperative that you keep your average investment yield above the average inflation rate and grab cost-of-living/inflation adjustments to any income source. Aside from a general level of inflation, there is specific price inflation for particular costs such as healthcare, property taxes, and food. Notice that none of these costs are optional and will strain any income level that does not keep up with the inflation rate.

Be aware that your tax preparer or CPA is not a tax strategist; nor is tax software. A tax strategist is someone who will examine your next five years of expected activity to coordinate and minimize your overall tax burden by aligning your spending, investments, business or real estate, plus your estate planning. Unfortunately for wage earners, there is little that can be done until you expand out into real estate or businesses.

Even with quite a bit of financial education, the first tax strategy session I ever attended in my early 20s left me in shock. The approach is very different from how most people think about their taxes (fill out the IRS forms and send a check). During this tax strategy meeting, there were several financial decisions that most people are never exposed to:

- How much income do you want to choose for yourself over the next few years?
- What type of income would you like that to be?
- What average tax rate would you like to pay?
- Among the favored tax-treatment items, are there any that you want to take advantage of this year that might not be available next year?
- How much insurance is needed to pay off a tax?
- How much money will you need to invest to reach a tax reduction goal?

As your financial stability improves so will your ability to take advantage of strategies like these to ramp up your income and net worth. Never forget that taxes are an anchor dragging on all of your finances and how you operate can dramatically minimize them. Seek expert advice for up-to-date tax strategies and never consider any illegal or illegitimate tactics.

Winning Concept #10

Always have insurance for unaffordable financial risks, such as life, health, auto, disability, and general liability.

It is a tragedy when someone is struck by the drama of life and then doubles that tragedy with a lack of insurance to pay for what is needed to recover from the situation.

There are too many personal stories where a predictable lack of insurance forced dreadful decisions and consequences for themselves or their families. It is my highest recommendation that you obtain independent professional advice, several price quotes, and enjoy the peace of mind of avoiding an unexpected financial crater that is irreversible.

In one example, an acquaintance passed away unexpectedly. He left his wife with no life insurance to cover the mortgage, car loans, boat loan, or college tuition for their two daughters. His health bills had consumed their savings from inadequate health insurance and her part-time income couldn't pay all the bills. Subsequently, their home was foreclosed, cars repossessed, and the family was forced to move in with her parents. Everything this family had worked to build up over 16 years was gone within six months due to a failure to buy adequate insurance policies that they could have easily afforded.

How much life insurance do you need? Financial planners will have a general rule such as 10 or 25 times your income; please ignore these estimates. Map out what you need by itemizing all of the costs. You must plan for: how much for funeral arrangements, debts or mortgage to be paid off, plus who is currently relying on you financially (a spouse, children, college costs, and possibly parents). The only other number to calculate is how much money you may want to provide so that a spouse does not have to work. This number could range from a year to a lifetime, depending on how much life insurance you can afford to buy. A term life insurance policy will always have an expiration date. You must match the date to correspond with your financial responsibilities. For example, if your children will be adults in 5 years, you do not need to pay more for a policy to last 10 years. The danger is getting a short-term policy when you have a long-term need and leave survivors financially exposed. There are many reasons that you may not be able to qualify for a new insurance policy later when your current one expires (for example, deteriorating health; or rates may have increased so high that you cannot afford an appropriate level of coverage).

Self-insurance is paying yourself in a separate account for the purpose of paying certain types of expenses on your own. This is a potential alternative to purchasing insurance because you get to keep your premium payments if you do not incur an event where you need this money. There are several types of insurance that quickly reach break-even calculations in favor of self-insurance: vision, dental, and often long-term care. For example, your dental insurance may cost you $1,000 per year. If instead you set this money aside into a self-insurance savings account for yourself, you will build up a reserve that may be more than enough to pay for many expensive dental procedures. Estimate some possible dental expenses and you can determine if it is more beneficial for you to self-insure rather than purchase insurance.

Please be aware that there is an extra insurance policy you should be considering once you enter your 50s: long-term healthcare for injury or illness. If your health ever deteriorated where you can no longer care for yourself, it can be a financial catastrophe to pay for permanent care that your health insurance does not cover after 100 days. There are options such as in-home care or nursing-home medical facilities with part-time or full-time care. This insurance becomes more expensive with age, but without it, your lifetime savings are at risk along with being forced to live in a government-run facility. (Visit a few local government-run nursing homes and compare to some private facilities to get an idea of conditions and care). Be aware that even long-term care insurance does not last long, most expire between 3 to 5 years which is why you should seriously consider self-insurance for this type of policy as well. Long-term care differs by state and county, plus it is a complicated topic that requires independent advice; look for elder law or elder-care experts. Some long-term healthcare issues are: how much in savings you'll expect to have; what are the government requirements; Medicaid rules; ask about any and all options. A last note: about half of U.S. states have

Filial Responsibility Statutes. These require spouses, children, and parents of indigent adults to pay for their care; you could get an invoice from the nursing home for the care of your parents. Although this is rarely enforced, as long-term care costs explode, these collections are expected to increase.[10]

Do not procrastinate on getting adequate insurance policies in force. It is a "Murphy's Law" that whichever insurance policy you are missing or is insufficient (even temporarily), will likely be the next financial event you encounter.

Winning Concept #11

Respectful partnership practices minimize the drama around family money decisions.

Financial problems are among the top reasons cited for divorce. Consider using the financial practices below to support your relationship:

1. Upfront Planning

When merging two households, it is also a financial merger of the income, assets, and debts; along with the spending habits and financial goals of both people. All of these need to be detailed for each other so they can be acknowledged, managed, and aligned to avoid inevitable conflict later on. Listening and working out differing goals and approaches can only take place after all of them are in the open for review. Love may not be enough to stay together if you have mutually exclusive financial goals or one of you continues to add unsustainable debts. It would be preferable to endure an unromantic moment of seeing each other's credit report rather than learn after the union about secret obligations and chronic problems.

Fairness in budgeting starts with comparing salaries. Use simple math to allocate costs: one partner's net pay divided by both partner's combined net pay is the ratio to determine how much money from each partner's income should be contributed to cover joint bills, savings, and investing. Some couples maintain separate accounts, and some couples can make it work for them, but this arrangement is ripe for feelings of distrust and unfairness to build up. I highly recommend that you have mostly joint accounts.

2. Transparency

Small financial secrets can grow into large financial secrets that can no longer be hidden and then trust is broken. The lesson is never permit a small financial secret into your relationship; openness in admitting losses or certain purchases may be painful in the short-term, but it is necessary for long-term harmony. You need two things to make transparency work. First, each of you must have some of your own spending money to use in any way that you want. Without this release valve, psychological pressure builds up where one or both of you feel financially controlled, resentful, trapped, judged, or disrespected. Everyone needs a little "off the books" money to buy things or even buy a surprise gift for your partner. Second, many couples find that financial autonomy can be kept by agreeing on a dollar threshold upon which the other partner must be consulted before a purchase; for example, a limit of $100, $250, or whatever is appropriate to your budget. However, keeping a secret account or credit card that your partner does not know about is a red-alarm that there are trust or control issues in the relationship that must be worked out. Aside from a little "off the books" spending, the rest of your financial life should be crystal clear to your partner. You cannot make joint decisions or take prudent action if one of you is in the dark about a critical problem. Another benefit of transparency is that two minds and networks are better than one at seeing potential problems, solutions, and opportunities.

Everyone makes money mistakes and many want to spend money on things that their partner would frown upon. These may be difficult to admit but adults own up to their mistakes, make compromises both can live with, and move on. Adults reveal spending problems to their partner because it can affect critical spending and planning for everyone in the family.

3. Allocation of Duties

Like all household duties, financial administration is one more item that needs to be done by someone. Whether one person does some, most, or all of the tasks, how they are allocated needs to be collaborative to make certain everything is being completed in a timely manner. If only one person is doing the financial tasks, it is still the individual responsibility of each partner to be aware of financial details and trends, to know what is going on, and to be occasionally involved. In the event the primary administrator is unable to perform the tasks because of illness or travel, the other partner needs to know how to perform these as well. Unlike other household tasks, finances have big consequences and you cannot go back in time if you were not involved for a few years and do not like what has happened.

INVESTING CONCEPTS

There is a universe of potential investment opportunities. This includes any number of activities where you are receiving income from an asset: a vending machine, a rental home, productive farm land, renting out your chainsaw or jewelry, buying a pallet of a product at a discount and selling them 1-by-1 at a higher price at a fair, etc. So never limit your thinking about investing to stocks or other exchange-traded securities. I am acquainted with a wealthy investor who has never bought anything related to stocks; he will only invest where he can have some direct control. So he primarily invests in small companies where he can control the operations, rental real estate, and sometimes, rare paintings. This type of thinking is not common, and he educated himself in these areas before he made any investments, but I want to highlight that there is no rule that investing is defined by exchange-traded instruments.

Despite all of the available options for investing, most people equate investing with stock ownership. This is passively investing in a small share of a publically traded business. Stock investing may have a place in your portfolio but realize where you are in the ownership line: last. The general path of publicly trading shares is that the business founder will never bring in a partner to reduce their ownership unless they absolutely have to. As someone who has worked in venture capital, I can assure you that the founders and money partners will never sell until they have extracted all of the value that they are capable of building for the company. So when the business is operating at its peak valuation and they cannot think of any way to make it more valuable, only then do they sell some of the company to the public in an IPO (initial public offering). Money managers buy this stock, add on their own ongoing fees for their investment fund, and then offer these to mutual fund investors. Although there are many reasons for an IPO, the path that I just described is common. Please notice that it is only when there is almost no more opportunity for profit that shares are made available to the general public.

However you decide for yourself that you want to invest, and whatever it is that you choose to invest in, there are several key concepts that you should keep in mind.

Investing Concept #1

Wealth is nothing more than the accumulation of money. It can only be started, built, and maintained by the portion of money that you receive and never spend.

Although wealth is a highly emotion-laden word, it is just an elaborate term for plain-old savings. If it helps you, replace the word wealth or portfolio with long-term savings to remove any distracting baggage. There are only two tasks for the accumulation of wealth: setting aside money into a bankroll and then investing this bankroll for growth. Sustainable wealth is only built upon sustained savings: you must continually add to the pile if you want it to grow into a meaningful amount of money. It is your assignment to increase your wealth over any time period that you care to track it: daily, monthly, quarterly, or annually. Fluctuating values may prevent this from actually occurring at each time interval, but you must consistently add new money and re-invest investment income so that an increase must assuredly occur over time.

The most important aspect of this first concept is accumulation. Each morning you inherit the cumulative financial decisions and actions that you have made in the past. The two greatest financial gifts that you bequeath to yourself each morning are good health and more money than you had the prior morning. Each day you can choose to continue the momentum and bequeath an improvement on these to yourself. Are you going to squander this morning's financial inheritance or improve upon it?

Everyone wants to find a loophole or stock tip to make them a quick fortune. It is deflating to finally learn that your wealth is mostly dependent on how much new money that you are adding to your own investments. For example, let's pretend that you found that fantasy investment which could quickly double in price, how much money do you currently have available to take advantage of this? $25, $2,500, $25,000? Let's assume that you can gather a lot of money like $25,000 and the investment actually doubles in a very short amount of time. Now what do you do with your original $25,000 plus the profit of $25,000? Do you now have enough to buy a private jet and retire in a mansion?

Not likely. You have to accumulate an incredible sum of money before it will throw off a lot of dividend and interest income on its own. Most of this money will come from your continual contributions. If you make sporadic contributions, then your investment bankroll is going to be significantly smaller than it could have been and you will have little capital to grow.

If you do not consistently allot new money for investing then you cannot take advantage of the most profitable asset building process: growing your net worth with the passage of time. The accumulation of your own contributions and investment returns on them can yield very large sums of money over time—but this is only available to those who continually add money that is never spent.

You earn some money, pay your expenses, and the money that is leftover is your capital and savings to potentially add to your wealth. If you have no capital or bankroll to invest, it is a spending failure on your part that only you can correct. This capital then needs to be employed by a capitalist to turn it into more money. Perhaps this capitalist is you. For example, in my teens I used money that I had saved to hire an aerial photographer to get images of two large university stadiums & campuses. After printing up some inventory I sold these photos to fanatical alumni for 10 times my cost. Did I spend any of this profit? Absolutely not; I grew my bankroll and used it to purchase some stock in a laser company. Did I spend any of the dividends from this stock? Absolutely not; I used it to increase my net worth by purchasing other investments. The discipline to grow your bankroll instead of spending and squandering your profit will assure a successful financial future. Finding active methods to increase your bankroll are not obvious, but they are available to anyone with financial ambition who is always scanning for them.

What is mathematically possible when putting aside money? It is possible to retire in only 7 years by saving 80% of your income. After 7 years, you will have piled up enough money so that you could withdraw 3% of it per year for possibly your lifetime. Any online retirement calculator can verify similar results. Although this is a very high savings rate, there are groups of people who collaborate online in trying to support each other with tactics in achieving a similarly quick and successful retirement.

Investing Concept #2

Treat every investment dollar with significance, as if it were the only extra dollar that you will ever have.

When you treat each investment dollar as meaningful, then you are more likely to educate yourself before you make an investment, monitor its progress and take decisive action when it is necessary to protect its survival and growth. This is the necessary perspective for investing success. To survive and thrive as an investor you actually need to have some investment dollars. This concept is so important that a multi-billionaire through investing has two similar investing rules: #1) Never Lose Money and #2) Never Forget Rule #1.[11] A flippant disrespect for your investing dollars will cause them to quickly disappear and you'll be left with nothing to show for your sacrifice that created the savings or your investing efforts.

No matter what the game, amateurs generally lose when they play against full-time professionals. In the game of investing, if you are playing casually long enough then you will end up donating much of your money to the professionals. If you lose your money in an investment, you have to earn that investing capital all over again from scratch. How many times can you afford to repeat this lesson? Invest wisely the first time in order to consistently move ahead instead of finding yourself attracted to high-risk gambles to play catch-up after yet another big loss.

Any place that you can put your money has risk. Even some place like cash under your mattress can be stolen or destroyed in a fire or flood. Every location for your money, whether for safekeeping or investing, must be thoughtful for it to remain safely in your control. A commonly used analogy is that you are a general and your money represents your soldiers. Any place that you direct your soldiers is a field of battle where your money is in harm's way. As the general, it is your objective to make sure all of your soldiers return and that they bring back additional soldiers with them (profit). Your soldiers depend solely on your capability and diligence for their safe return and success at bringing back additional soldiers. If money is lost it is solely your responsibility and your due diligence failure; it is not the fault of any actual investment.

If you are investing in anything—whether it is a strategy, a tactic, or particularly a direct investment, it is only skepticism, knowledge, and experience that will keep your money safe. There are no risky or safe investments, the only safety for your money will come from your self-education, self-training, monitoring, and follow-through. No one has a vested interest in your money as much as you do and it is solely up to you to give it the best opportunity to grow.

Any investor that is not a severe skeptic will not have money to manage for very long. One of the roles of an investor is to be a persistent skeptic, asking due-diligence questions such as "based on what," "how do you know that," "prove it," "exactly how did you calculate that number," "show me the building," "show me all the fine print," "what is guaranteed and by whom, what is their credit rating?" These probing questions will reveal what is true and what is false about a potential investment. You need these answers, in an ongoing basis, to make prudent investment decisions.

It is unfortunate that the IRS uses a tax label called "passive investment income." Salespeople use this term as a benefit of their particular investment but the reality is there is no such thing as passive income or a passive investment. It is a concept with universal appeal, but like a mythical creature, nothing we can experience in reality. All income-producing assets must be created and managed. Those that are not managed eventually disappear, or worse, become liabilities that lose money.

Investing regulations require licensed professionals to determine from your experience what level of risk and type of investing is appropriate for you. This is to protect the brokerage firm from legal liability; but in my opinion this approach is 180° backwards. First you should determine your financial goals, and then determine what investments or strategies are needed to get you there. Only then do you raise your knowledge so that those are not risky investments for you. Do not invest according to your risk tolerance; intelligently increase your tolerance to match the investing methods you need to reach your goals.

No matter what your career or profession may be there is one task that you must undertake and cannot entirely outsource—asset manager. You must manage your own investments or manage your money manager who does this on your behalf. This is why you cannot avoid the skill of investing skepticism.

Different levels of financial freedom or a comfortable early retirement are only reserved for asset managers. I sincerely hope that you decide to become one of them. If you refuse your duty as an asset manager then you are left with only two net-worth building options: paying down debt or putting money into some poor-performing savings account. If you do not have any money, then make it and save it. If you have no investing education, then go get it. If you have no time to learn, make room for it. It is an error to believe that you have to pay off all of your debts first, do not procrastinate your asset-manager role by waiting a moment longer to allocate money into investments.

Investing Concept #3

The majority of your investments must make regular cash payments.

Let's start at your end target—why do you have investments at all? To have the ability to spend money that is not earned income. Investments are not spendable until they either produce income or are sold. If your investment does not pay any income then you must start selling off some of it to have spendable money. This liquidation permanently reduces your principal balance, making you poorer. If you do this during retirement, it begins the possibility of running out of money when you are least able to earn more money.

A goal as an investor is to replace your earned income with investment income. There are many goals that you may have as an investor but I recommend that they should have less importance than replacing your earned income until you have done so. There will be a time when you are unable or unwilling to keep working for earned income. How are you going to pay your bills aside from selling what you own and hoping that you do not run out? In my opinion, retirement plans that call for selling off what you have built up is similar to choosing a financial crash landing and hoping that you survive the crash. A retirement study by William Bengen concluded that a retiree's portfolio would likely survive for 30 years if only 4% of the balance were withdrawn per year (and the 4% increases by the rate of inflation each year thereafter).[12] This 4% rule is based on many assumptions and is only meant as a starting point in your financial planning. This 4% rule may be your retirement planning Plan B, but it is my best advice that your Plan A for retirement should be to never spend the principal amount. Once you start liquidating your investments, you are subject to a principal called "the sequencing of returns." This means that a few ill-timed bear markets can implode your portfolio so much that you'll run out of money decades too soon. If owning investments with regular cash payments is where you will eventually end up, then why not build your expertise and capability around this from the start of your investing career?

Although I have investments that do not make regular

cash payments, these are small investments for speculation based on unusual circumstances. Until you have acquired the knowledge and experience of investing for capital gains, your portfolio will grow far more resiliently if it receives regular dividend and interest payments.

There are 6 favorable consequences when your investments produce cash distributions:

1. It starts the payback of your principal investment which reduces your risk and increases your rate of return. When you put your hard-earned money into someone else's hands, you want that money back as fast as possible. It does not matter whether the return is in the form of interest, dividends, principal payments, tax deductions, or other financial benefits. As your money is returned, the amount of your original investment that remains at risk is diminished, which reduces your cost-basis in the investment and increases your future returns on the remaining amount of money you have at risk.

2. It starts the mathematical mechanism of compounding your investment return—earning interest upon interest. Until you receive cash back from an investment it is not available to compound. If your investment is not compounding with cash distributions, then it must compound internally on its own to make up for the opportunity cost that you are missing out on. It is a rare achievement for any passive investment to produce a high level of internal compounding over a long period of time. Even the most successful and legendary companies rarely outperform the market for more than a 5-to-10-year stretch.

3. Payments from investments act as a buffer to fluctuations in the value of the investment itself. In the possibility that there is a loss or no capital gain to be had on the principal of the investment, then the payments of dividends and interest may become your sole positive return on the investment.

4. It creates the financial capacity to further diversify by purchasing additional income-producing assets of a different type. Dividend and interest payments can be directed into new investments that is more difficult or impossible for nonpaying investments to do. The more your money is spread into different individual investments and classes of assets, the more stable your investment portfolio value will become.

5. It adds consistency to the returns of your investments. In the mathematics of portfolio investing, the consistency of returns is more important than the rate of return. For example, two different investments can have the exact same average return over 10 years; however the investment that has more consistency (less variability) will be worth far more than the other one. In many cases, the more variable investment will never catch up to the consistent investment (in the story of the Tortoise and the Hare, you want your passive investments to be like the Tortoise, making steady profitable progress).

6. Investments that have to make regular payments are more likely to be legitimate. The investment world has its share of crooks along with people who turn to fraud to cover up losses. Since this is the reality of the investing arena, you must address it by performing ongoing due diligence or requiring regular audits. An investment that makes reasonable regular payments has less flexibility to create deceit.

Each time that you make an investment solely for a capital gain, you need the possibility to make several investments that mitigate your investment risk. This mitigation of your risk is part of investing mathematics and you have heard the term many times—diversification. Diversification can be easily explained by using a casino as an example. You enter a casino with your lifetime savings of $1,000 and purchase a single $1,000 chip at the roulette table. You put your chip on your lucky number 7, but the ball falls on the slot for number 31. All of your capital is now gone. You have just permitted a single speculation to preclude you from all future gambling until you can find a way to get more money. You fired your 1,000 employees of dollars that could have been earning money for you and generations to come. You busted and went broke in a manner that anyone knowledgeable about gambling could have anticipated. It is imprudent to put all of your investment money at risk for a capital gain without the diversification of several attempts. How many attempts? That depends on the particular odds where you placed your bet around the roulette betting table. The same concept applies outside of a casino; the odds, risk, and reward are different for speculating with raw land, a partnership to drill an oil well, or buying the stock of a fast-growing technology company. The higher the probability of success and the more stable the intrinsic value, the fewer investing attempts are needed to minimize your risk of going broke.

Is this concept about cash payments just my personal-pet theory? What do the professionals do; the ones who have a fiduciary responsibility to be legally prudent with their money management? You will find that insurance companies, pension funds, and endowments regularly have a minimum of 50% of their money invested with income-producing investments. What happens to those fiduciaries that have few or no income-producing investments? They do not last long.

I attended a meeting with a wealthy active investor when he was being pitched a large local real estate deal. The brokers were confident that he would invest in their private placement because the investment was expected to make 300% in roughly 5 years. After the presentation, the investor's first question was, "Why are there no payments throughout the 5 years? The 300% capital gain is a speculation. I require quarterly payments from anyone that has my money. Since I won't let you return my own money back to me, what are you going to do to earn money over those 5 years so that you can make profit payments to me?" The brokers were dumbfounded that anyone would possibly turn down a potential 300% gain in a few years. Their business plan had no earning capability to make payments so the investor turned them down flat. While the poor investing "experts" were focusing on the return on investment, the successful investor insisted on a prudent return *of* his investment through regular cash payments.

The goal of your portfolio is to increase your cash flow and increase its value. There are three investing modes to achieve this goal:

1. Aggressive gains
2. Defensive protection
3. Neutrality of cash reserves

Among these three investing modes, investments that make regular cash distributions can accomplish all three at once. However, an investment without cash distributions can only perform one mode, even if it succeeds. The foundation of your portfolio will always be investments making regular cash payments, so it should be the focus of every investor to know the most about these types of investments. Re-investing the cash flow from investments builds the long-term sustainability of your portfolio and can be a source of funds for a few small purchases that are strictly for aggressive capital gains.

Investing Concept #4

Continually use competition with your investments, advisors, and strategies to weed out poor performers and migrate your money toward the best performers.

This concept can be explained by an old vending machine tactic. The owner of vending machines at many different locations wants to improve the business income. So the owner pulls the machines from the lowest earning locations and places them at new locations. The owner continues to log what each machine is earning to rotate the worst of them into new locations. After 5 years of culling the lowest performers, the business has amazingly doubled its income even though it has the exact same number of vending machines. This same tactic can be applied to your investments and investment advisors. A family friend always has three investment advisors. Each quarter, he reviews their performance and reduces the amount of money that he has with the worst performer. If the worst performer continues to underperform the other two advisors, he or she is replaced with a new advisor.

Similarly, the institutions that manage stock indexes also cull the weak and shrinking company valuations and replace them with strong and growing valuations. The major indexes do this all the time: Dow Jones Industrial Average, Standard & Poor's 500 Index, NASDAQ Index, Wilshire 5000 Total Market Index, etc. This culling is part of the reason why stock indexes eventually move upward. If you cannot find investments or better performing advisors, then invest in stock and bond indexes by the cheapest way possible.

Professional investors of any type are always scanning for new opportunities that will provide better returns. Similarly, you should periodically see if there are investments or advisors that may ratchet up your portfolio performance. Do your research, test the investment with a small amount of money, and only migrate money in small doses. Never concentrate too much of your portfolio into a single investment or asset class.

STOCK INVESTING MECHANICS

How to Invest in
the Stock Market

You should be aware of a simple, easy, and profitable strategy for stock investing, and that is the **Allocate and Rebalance Strategy.** This strategy is so sound that many well-respected economists, finance professors, money managers, and business leaders use this exact method (or something very similar) for the majority of their personal investment portfolio. For many of these people, it is their only investing method. If you should decide not to use it, at least you will know what everyone else is talking about and have a reference point to validate if your stock investing strategy is performing better than this or not.

The year in which someone has entered the finance profession is typically revealed by what average return rate they reference for stock investing. Most say the market will earn 10% to 12% per year on average, but I can assure you that these refer to cherry-picked time frames just after a large downturn to present you an unrealistically high-return rate. The most reliable data for the U.S. stock market goes back 140 years, and over this period the stock market advanced by an average of 8.9% per year.[13] This historical return rate is much lower than many financial advisors claim it is, plus it is before taxes are applied. Still, there is no better passive investment class to grow your bankroll and stay ahead of inflation than investing in a diversified portfolio of stocks over a 20-year period.

The easiest way to take advantage of the upward march of the stock market is to own a low-cost stock index fund. Over the long-term, indexes beat 92% of all actively managed stock funds and money managers.[14]

The best way to invest in an index fund is through the originator of low-cost index investing, Vanguard Investments founded by John Bogle. Bogle has written several books on investing and he focuses on the individual investor making money instead of their money managers.

Simply owning a U.S. stock index is, unfortunately, a volatile investment. It is therefore recommended that you diversify by owning two other broad index funds: a foreign stock index and a short-term bond index. Your allocation of invested funds should be allocated among three indexes: U.S. stocks, foreign stocks, and U.S. bonds. An allocation among these three is all that you need. You can find fancier financial profiles with over 30 different sub-types of investments, but they offer little advantage and a lot more complexity over just holding those 3 investments.

Which stock index?

Choose any broad stock index. There are many narrow stock indexes, such as only retail companies or biotech companies, or mid-sized companies—you do not want these sub-components but an index that includes a large basket of diversified companies. Among the broad stock market indexes, academic finance research has not yet settled which one is best. For example, a growth index will outperform a general index when the market is going up but then underperform when the market is going down.

How much should you hold in domestic vs. international stocks?

Pension and endowment managers normally target 30% foreign vs. 70% domestic, but can go as high as 40% foreign vs. 60% domestic. Again, finance research has not yet settled this. For some periods of time the U.S. market outperforms foreign stock markets and vice-versa.

How much should you hold in stocks vs. bonds?

The concept of diversification is the only "free lunch" in finance. Briefly, a diversified portfolio reduces your risk by owning so many items that when one of them falls in value there are others that will have risen in value as well. Together, they are more stable and adding bonds to a stock portfolio further reduces the variability of a portfolio. Even though bonds do not perform as profitably as stocks over the long term, the bonds produce higher interest income and reduce the volatility to make your portfolio balance far more stable. Finance research has not definitively proven how much to hold in bonds, but allocating between 20% to 80% into bonds is optimal for individual investors. The higher the bond ratio the more conservative your portfolio results will become. Many advisers recommend using your age as a moving allocation percentage for bonds (be aware there are many approaches to determine this percentage: your age, 120 minus your age, and changing retirement target-date fund calculations.) As you age, you'll have a higher fixed-income ratio to slowly stabilize your portfolio as you get closer to needing the money for spending. Since people are living longer than they did 50 years ago, over the last 15 years more studies are showing that using your age for your bond allocation is too conservative. Actuarial studies are predicting that people can expect to live 20–30 years after they retire so a little more exposure to higher stock returns is needed to maintain their style of living for such a long period of time. So instead of using your age, I recommend that you use between 70% to 80% of your current age as your bond allocation.

It is important to only buy a short-term bond fund. Bonds mature or expire at a date in the future when the principal balance is returned. Bond fund managers can choose bonds that expire in a few weeks to several decades away. What is critical for investors is that bond prices are very sensitive to changes in interest rates. The further away an expiration date is for a bond, the more sensitive it is to these interest rate changes. So a sharp uptick in general interest rates will drop the value of a long-term bond fund very sharply. This is a risk that you want to minimize by only holding short-term bond funds. Another risk of medium and long-term bond funds is that when the markets get choppy, investors may exit the fund with redemptions and force the fund to sell bonds at a loss. I would advise not to hold a bond fund with a duration (average maturity date) of 5 years or more. The slight increase in yield is not worth the potential sharp drop in value. Note that this advice is strictly for a bond fund, if you are purchasing individual bonds then my advice is quite different (An individual bond is a loan to a company, but to the investor it is a cash-flow-timing mechanism to fund your cash requirements.)

Your portfolio allocation summary:

1. Choose a short-term U.S. bond index fund.

(This index fund must hold only investment-grade credit bonds, not higher yielding junk bonds, fallen-angel bonds, frontier-economy bonds, etc. that have poorer credit). Allocate between 20–70% of your portfolio to this bond fund, using 75% of your current age the percentage for your allocation. Whatever percentage you choose to allocate for your bond index fund, your remaining balance of money will all go toward stock market index funds.

2. Choose a broad U.S. stock market index fund.
Allocate 65% of your money that you have allocated to all stocks to a U.S. stock market index fund.

3. Choose a broad foreign stock market index fund,
(Not a fund that invests in only one country or continent.) The foreign stock market index fund is an index fund excludes U.S.-based companies. Allocate 35% of your money that you have allocated to all stocks into this foreign stock market fund.

For a sample exercise, if you are now 35 years old:

- Bond index fund allocation = 75% times 35, or 26%
- The remainder of your portfolio for stocks = 100% - 26%, or 74%
- U.S. stock index fund allocation = 65% times 74%, or 48%
- Foreign stock index fund allocation = 35% times 74%, or 26%

So your 3-fund portfolio for a 35-year-old would have these target allocations:

1. Short-term bond index fund 26%
2. U.S. stock index fund 48%
3. Foreign stock index fund 26%

Rebalance Your Portfolio

As the markets move your actual allocations will drift above and below your original target allocations. How and when should you rebalance to get your actual portfolio back to your target allocations? Numerous academic studies have been done and the best answer so far (for individual investors) is once a year. If you rebalance more often, your transaction costs increase so much that it lowers your overall return. Many other rebalance methods have been tested, such as a percentage above/below your target; rebalance half-way back to your target; daily adjustments, etc. None of these, so far, are definitively better than just rebalancing once a year.

The primary driver of your portfolio gains will be your money that is allocated to stocks. When the stock market falls, your stock allocation percentage drops, and to rebalance your portfolio you would sell some of your bond index funds to buy more stock index funds. In this case, you are using your bond index money as a reserve of money that is ready and available to buy stocks at a lower price. Contrarily, when the stock market advances and goes above your target allocation, you would rebalance by selling stocks at a high price to replenish your bond-index reserve. In this manner the stock market is a pump that slowly moves up and down and you utilize your bond-index reserve to collect profits and then fund future purchases for the next oscillation of the stock market.

Assuming that you are regularly adding new money to your investments as well, you would add this new money solely to the index fund that is the lowest below its target allocation at that time. If it is a stock index fund, then you are buying stocks relatively cheap, and if it is your bond index fund, then you are buying bonds relatively cheap.

What about starting a portfolio from scratch, does it matter when you enter the market?

Although many academics say that no one can time the market correctly or that it does not matter in the long term, I believe you should take a look at the choppy 15-year chart below for yourself. There are two +40% price drops that you would have suffered if you had bought in at the price tops. Do you really want to take the risk that you might be making all of your purchases at a price peak?

S&P 500 Stock Index from 1997 to 2012:

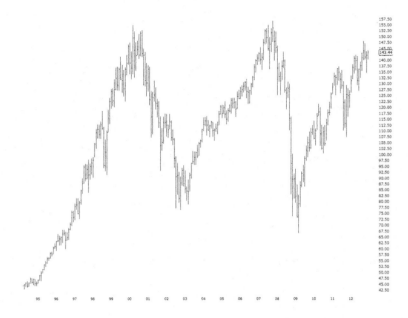

(Courtesy of FreeStockCharts.com)

My best advice is to scale into your positions. Do this by dividing your portfolio by 16. Each quarter over the next 4 years you will add these 1/16th portions to your investment selections. If you do this for less than 4 years you risk buying all of your investments around a market peak, and if you spread out your purchases for longer than 4 years, you risk missing too much of the uptrends that you are hoping to profit from.

There are other timing methods for adding new money into stocks that you may want to consider. For example, add less money to stocks when the U.S. Federal Reserve is raising short-term interest rates; add less money to stocks when the S&P 500 Index 200-day moving average is moving down. Or add less money to stocks when the S&P 500 Price/Earnings ratio is above its historical average of 15.5.

10 Years of the S&P 500 Index with a 200-day moving average line:

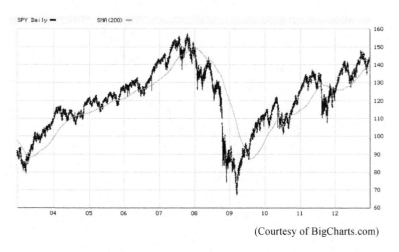

(Courtesy of BigCharts.com)

The Price/Earnings Ratio of the S&P 500 Index from 1890:

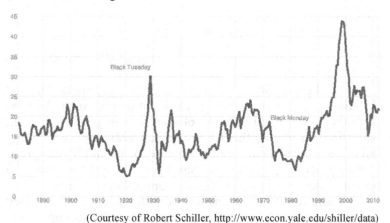

(Courtesy of Robert Schiller, http://www.econ.yale.edu/shiller/data)

    Today, there are two types of index investments: mutual funds and ETFs. For new investors, a mutual fund is easier to buy, sell, and administer while ETFs trade on an exchange just like stocks. In general, mutual funds incur annual expenses of 1–2% per year and are far greater than the annual expense of an ETF. However, trading ETFs also involves paying commissions every time you buy or sell them. So you must pay a commission each time you rebalance your portfolio; but more frequently, each time that you add new money to your investments. Investment expenses and transaction costs reduce your returns and should always be minimized. Over a few decades even a small expense of 1% makes a very dramatic reduction in your investment balance. So let's map out which type of index fund may be better for you. For example, if you have an investment portfolio of $10,000 in mutual funds, you are losing 2% per year to expenses, or $200. If, instead, you had $10,000 in ETFs and added new money each month, then you might have to pay: $10 per commission every month, or $120; $30 for 3 commissions to rebalance 3 funds once a year, for $30. The commissions would cost you $150 per year.

In this example, you are better off holding ETFs instead of mutual funds even though your account is just $10,000. Mutual fund expenses and commission rates change, but now you can calculate for yourself which direction will lower your annual costs. For most account sizes, ETFs are cheaper and so they will provide less of a drag on your investing returns over your investing time horizon.

For most people without much interest in investing, this chapter may be all that you need for your entire investing career. In just a few pages you have a task list of what you need to do, and after it is set up, you only have one action to take a year. Most people would prefer to own a single investment and never have to think about investing again. Well, this is as close as it gets and it is relatively easy, statistically proven, and profitable over long time-frames.

Some educated investors point out that, "Isn't the Allocate and Rebalance Method what Retirement Target Date Funds do?" The answer is yes and no. Yes, they attempt it, but you do not know exactly what you are getting over time. The range of allocations varies greatly between brokerage firms, funds change their formulas based on recent results only to get stung with poorer performance, some of their changes are due to competition and not proven finance research. In my opinion, these target date funds are a simple way to manage your money, but the increase in management fees and periodic formula changes make them less desirable than doing it on your own.

Investing Style Cliques

Even though you may have your own investing style, has it performed as well as the Allocate and Rebalance Strategy? No matter how you choose to invest, you are going to read and hear about many other ways to invest your money. The investing world is chock-full of new sales pitches, theories, and techniques. Here are some of the more popular ones that you may come across:

1. "You should buy individual stocks on your own" Sales Pitch. They will claim that short-term investing is reckless gambling so you should invest in individual stocks by yourself for the long-term just like the billionaire Warren Buffett. They will advise you to buy shares in the companies of the products that your children are begging you to buy for their birthday. They say it so easy and simple to make a +25% returns each year by investing in undervalued stocks. The bible for this group is a 1934 book titled, *Security Analysis,* co-written by an economist, Benjamin Graham. Graham was a value investor whose most successful student to date has been money-manager Warren Buffett. It is incredibly difficult to outperform the stock market indexes. Millions try to do this, but very few people have consistently been able to achieve it.

2. "You are a tiny outsider" Sales Pitch. They will claim that their firm has access to inside connections, brilliant analysts, billions of dollars under management, and supercomputers with sophisticated software that produce huge returns that you cannot possibly get on your own. "Invest your money with my cabal of smart insiders and we will make you a fortune." This is decades-old Wall Street sales material but the returns simply do not materialize for retail customers.

3. "Learn my new trading system" Sales Pitch. They will say: "Attend my seminar, buy my software &

books, subscribe to my newsletter, and I'll show you how to make huge profits by using X." Where X can be price chart patterns, seasonal spreads, moon phases, proprietary indicators, institutional trades, penny stocks, earnings projections, forex robots, analyst ratings, pre-IPOs, potential merger targets, Elliott waves, cycle analysis, oscillating indicators, stock splits, earnings pre-announcements, yet another new form of candlestick charts, new enterprise value calculations, delta-neutral options, secret Gann calculations, covered-calls, neural network programming, binary options, tape reading, Fibonacci numbers—you name it. These products and services are sold to inexperienced beginners by vendors whose primary income is rarely trading profits. Some of these offer value to investors, and I know people who make their living trading from what they have learned, but history has shown that the vast majority of systems sold do not make money for their customers.

I know people who make their living solely by trading exchange-traded instruments. However, the trade craft required to make money by doing this in all kinds of market conditions is very difficult to achieve. Be aware that the majority of short-term traders lose money just like gamblers with a system trying to beat the casino. Crafting your own profitable trading method is a tremendous undertaking of detailed research, psychological conditioning, and ongoing development.

Proven Investing Theories

There are many other sales pitches for extra-profitable returns, but are any of them valid? Possibly, but it is likely that they would quickly be managing a lot of money with everyone clamoring to have him or her managing their money. My best advice for your consideration is to know the passive stock investing tactics that have been proven over time with the most academic evidence:

1. Stock Diversification (1959), Risk reduction with

increasing number of securities.[15]

2. Asset Allocation (1986), Reduce the variation of your portfolio return by allocating a percentage of money into stocks, bonds, and cash.[16]

3. Low-Cost Stock Indexing (1976), Vanguard Mutual Funds.[17]

4. Low-Cost Stock Index ETFs (1993), Standard & Poor's ETFs.[18]

5. Asset Location (2004), Place investments that are taxed at high ordinary-tax rates in retirement accounts and place investments taxed at low capital-gains-tax rates in regular after-tax accounts.[19]

Each year there are new financial investments and strategies, plus old strategies are revived that work well in certain rare conditions, but work horribly the rest of the time. Most of these never catch on, but every once in a while some method becomes popular and it is studied closely to determine if it may offer any risk/return advantage to be added to a portfolio.

Until a new improvement comes along, the Allocation and Rebalance Method for stock investing is one that you should seriously consider.

"Tell Me About Gold."

One of the most common investing questions I am asked is about the ownership of physical gold. The answers and comments below are my humble opinions:

1) Is Owning Gold an Investment?
Absolutely not.
A bar of gold in your hand generates no interest income, no dividend income, and its ownership does not capitalize any business activity. Yes, you can use gold for speculation just like you can with anything that has value: raw land, rare paintings, baseball cards, or comics. Simply because an object has value does NOT make it an intrinsic investment, let alone a wise and prudent purchase for speculation.

2) Is Gold Money?
No; it hasn't been transactional money for a very long time.
Take a few grains of gold that you panned from a stream and try to pay your restaurant bill. If someone on the street offered you a coin that looked like a 1 oz. gold coin, would you pay them the spot price of gold for it or would you presume it was counterfeit or some kind of scam? No form of physical gold is routinely accepted for transactions today (the only place is a pawnshop experienced in gold and silver), so it is not fungible like cash for transactions.

3) Is Gold a Currency?
Yes, it is; a metallic currency without a nationality.
A currency can be defined as a portable store of value used for exchange. It is my opinion that gold is a currency; however, it has several features that make it one of the most cumbersome currencies:

- It is a physical object so to own it you have to transport it, store it, insure it, and periodically have it physically counted.
- You must have it assayed before you buy it to

discover its authenticity.
- You must have it assayed again before you sell it to prove its authenticity.
- It is heavy and malleable (a bad combination).
- If your gold is in the form of a collectible item, then it will also need an appraisal by an expert.
- Depending on the gold object or contract you are trading there can also be an expensive bid/ask spread on each transaction.

All of these traits make gold something inconvenient and expensive to own. However, what makes gold so attractive is that politicians cannot destroy its value. Gold has been a desirable store of value since it was discovered 6,000 years ago[20], and it has been used in coins since 610 BC.[21] Meanwhile, paper currencies that are backed by nothing eventually approach worthlessness. How would you like to wake up in the morning to find that politicians have reduced the value of your cash by 30% to over 90%? This has happened during the last couple decades in Belarus, Iceland, Russia, Argentina, Mexico, and several other countries. Expectations are rising that the next in line for devaluations are Greece, Ireland, Portugal, Italy, Spain, along with a possibility of the U.S., France, Japan, Austria, and Britain. Iran's currency lost 57% in only 8 days in 2012.[22] Do you believe a currency devaluation cannot occur in the U.S.? The federal government devalued the U.S. dollar to gold by 69% in January, 1934.[23] The Federal Reserve has printed $2.11 trillion dollars from 2009 through the first part of 2012, which must eventually have a negative effect on the value of the dollar.[24]

4) Is Gold a Hedge Against Inflation?
Sometimes.
Over very long periods of time, the correlation between inflation and gold is low. Using over 80 years of U.S. Federal Reserve data, there is almost no correlation between changes in inflation and the price of gold. It is only during periods of rising inflation that gold acts as a positive hedge against inflation.[25] Although the financial world is littered with reasons why an investor should hold some gold, it is usually dead money in a portfolio unless inflation is rising.

5) Should Every Portfolio Hold Gold?
No; many people do not have currency exposure that needs to be hedged.

First, there is only a single period of time when anyone would want to own the currency of gold. This is when there is upward pressure on the price of gold from the effect of "negative real interest rates". This is an economic term that I will explain. If interest rates are at 2% but inflation is at 5% then your inflation-adjusted return is not 2% but 2% minus 5% or -3%. So although you are earning 2% on your money, inflation is taking away 5% of it, leaving you with -3% of your purchasing power. Your inflation-adjusted return is -3% and "real" is the economic term for this inflation adjustment. So when inflation-adjusted interest rates are negative, investors are losing purchasing power and becoming poorer (even though they are receiving interest income). This is the time when investors migrate toward any kind of stronger currency, including gold, putting upward pressure on the price of gold. So investors watch to see if real interest rates are positive or negative. When they are negative, investors start to buy gold to maintain their purchasing power.

Gold Price with Real Interest Rates as a Buy/Sell Signal:

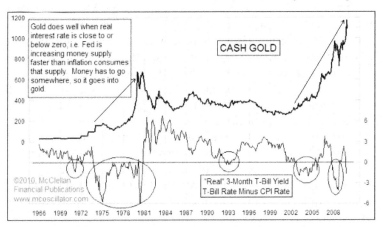

(Courtesy of The McClellan Market Report, McOscillator.com)

The recent annualized consumer price index is around 3%, which is far greater than the 3-month T-bill yield of 0.05%, making the real interest rate .0005-.02 = -0.0295, a negative real interest rate.[26] So now is an appropriate time to own any number of stronger currencies, including gold. Since 2005, the average inflation rate has been greater than the yield on short-term money (most of the time) which currently makes gold an attractive currency to hold. Coincidentally, since 2005 the price of gold has risen 300% in dollar terms. When the inflation rate is lower than the yield on short-term money, real interest rates will be positive again and there will be downward pressure on the price of gold. This is when the price of gold normally goes down or sideways and you do NOT want to own gold during this period.

Second, if you determine that now is an appropriate time to own gold (inflation rate is greater than short term interest rates), how do you decide how much gold to own? Common financial planning advice is that 5–10% of your investment portfolio should be in gold. However, their reasoning is only for diversification, just blindly owning gold all the time. If you want that role in your investment portfolio, that is your choice, but I would never advise this. Gold is a very-poor performing asset over long periods of time; particularly when inflation is falling or low.

If there is high inflation, hyper-inflation, or a currency devaluation, what do you actually have at risk that the politicians and central banks are destroying? All of the assets that you own (home, car, boat, stocks, etc.) are priced in U.S. dollars. If inflation rises, then so will the paper-dollar price of your assets. But there is one asset that cannot re-price in inflated dollars: the actual dollars, the paper currency that you own. Just like melting ice, any dollars that you are holding will fall in value as you hold them. This category includes cash, savings accounts, checking accounts, money market accounts, treasury bills or certificates of deposit, and other short-term investments. These are liquid, or near liquid, forms of currency that become worth less as inflation rises or the currency loses value. All of this money that you have has the potential risk of losing purchasing power by the tax of inflation, hyper-inflation, or currency devaluation.

Now that you understand what you have at risk, it is my advice that these forms of money that you own and are NOT planning to spend or invest in the next few years are your candidates to replace with gold. Basically, gold should not be part of your investments, it should only replace some of your savings that you do not plan on spending in the next few years. Instead of holding U.S. dollars that are falling in value, you would be holding your savings in the currency of gold. You could choose any percentage of this cash (that you do not plan on spending or investing over the next few years), but I would recommend that you hold between 25% to 75% of this amount in gold. Why not 100%? Because the price of gold varies greatly, its correlation to inflation/devaluation varies, and it is not a perfect hedge. For the money that you want hedged, gold is one of a few instruments you can use for protection. There are others such as inflation-adjusted securities, inflation-protected treasuries, floating-rate funds, and more. If your biggest concern is a government default or devaluation, then holding gold or other currencies is more appropriate. But if your biggest concern is persistent inflation, then inflation-adjusted securities may be more appropriate to hold. You can also benefit from high inflation by borrowing money with fixed-rate long-term loans because the principal and payments melt in value with inflation while your wages, rental or business income can advance with inflation.

An important consideration when holding gold is the current level of interest rates because: there is no such thing as a free hedge. When interest rates are very low, the opportunity cost of moving your money from savings accounts or bank CDs into gold is almost nothing. But if interest rates are medium to high, then the interest you could have been earning while you hold gold becomes a meaningful amount of money. If you could earn 7% in a money market account, then you may want to hold less gold as you could garner a decent return without taking any gold-price risk.

6) How Should I Buy Gold?
The simple answer is cheaply; as close to the spot price of gold as possible.
Preferably in a form that is the most liquid and most recognized for trade. I recommend the 1 oz. gold American Eagle coin. You can get these from any local coin dealer or comparison shop from reputable online dealers. The long answer to this question is that it depends on how much homework, time, and effort that you want to put into it. If you want your gold held offshore there are Australian certificate accounts or if you want

to reach for extra return, you could get more expertise to buy collectable gold coins. If you travel to Asia, Hong Kong offers gold coins at a very low markup over the spot price of gold. There are two places where you should avoid buying gold: an allocated gold account from a bank or investment bank (across the globe, banks periodically get caught charging customers storage costs for non-existent gold that investors had paid for), the second is auction websites; although reputable dealers sell here as well, they have been a haven for stolen and counterfeit coins. If you choose to buy bars of gold bullion there is also extra paperwork. What about gold and silver ETFs that you can buy just like a stock? I have owned them in the past as a temporary speculation, but the more I learn about their settlement risk, the less confidence I have in owning these securities. If your gold is not in your hand, then what you own, if anything, is another risk that you do not want to take. This risk also includes bank safety deposit boxes for a few reasons: they are not insured, states are getting more aggressive at taking "dormant accounts" as unclaimed funds to reduce their deficits, some fear confiscation from the U.S. Patriot Act, or remember that owning gold in the U.S. was outlawed from 1933 until 1974 and could be passed again. Instead, put your valuables at facilities whose only business is "secure storage" or "private safe-deposit boxes."

7) Do You Own Any Gold?
Yes.
But let me repeat that your only money at risk for inflation/ devaluation is your cash/short-term cash-equivalent money that you do not plan on spending in the next few years. Of this amount of money, I have about 50% in precious metals and 50% in inflation-adjusted bonds. The precious metals that I own are coins that are strictly 1 oz. gold American Eagles and 1 oz. silver American Eagles; I have them both for a little diversification. I prefer these coins for precious metals because they are the most recognized, physical, easily portable, and they are private transactions. Remember: I do not own this gold for speculation, but for possessing something of value in the face of trillions in unfunded and unsustainable U.S. debts that will continue to weaken the U.S. currency. It is an insurance hedge for currency inflation/devaluation that will fluctuate in

price but its purpose is not profit but maintaining some value to hedge against a depreciating currency.

8) When Will You Sell Your Gold?

When short-term interest rates rise above the inflation rate.
As shown in the prior chart, when the 3-month U.S. Treasury bill rate goes above the CPI-reported inflation rate, and stays there, then I will begin selling my gold (and any other precious metals). At this inflexion point, history has shown that the price of gold normally falls in price during this scenario. The reasoning is that when investors receive a positive return to hold local paper currency, they abandon gold and transfer that money to places where it earns a return, such as money market accounts and CDs, etc. Precious metal prices have had huge swings and volatility so you do not want to own them when their economic fundamentals do not favor a price increase.

9) Are Gold Charts Useful?

Yes, the price of real estate, stocks, oil, etc. divided by the price of gold are helpful barometers of relative value.
Charts that cross two items, such as these below, are a useful addition to determine what is relatively overpriced or underpriced. Just glancing at some of these long-term charts reveals if you are buying near the top of a bubble or selling near the bottom of a price collapse. I look at these a few times a year as another reference point on changes in relative value. As you can see, trends can last for years to give you plenty of time to evaluate your positions.

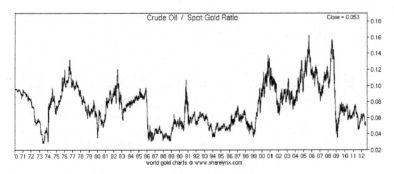

(Courtesy of Nick Laird at ShareLynx.com)

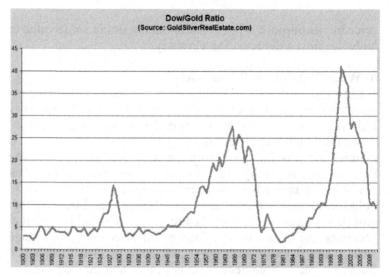

(Courtesy of Nick Laird at ShareLynx.com)

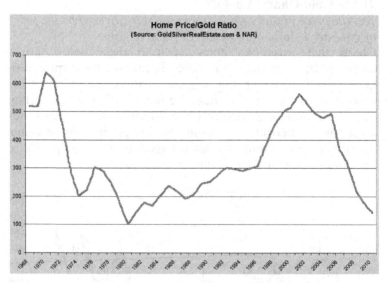

(Courtesy of Nick Laird at ShareLynx.com)

10) Anything Else I Should Know About Gold?

Yes, don't go crazy and catch "gold fever."

For every logical argument for buying or selling gold there are a dozen arguments from the gold fanatics that you should hoard all the gold you can. It is easy to find perennial gold fans who are hyper-alert for the coming political and economic apocalypse that is always just around the corner. Some of these apocalyptic arguments have been waiting to materialize for hundreds of years, and in the U.S. since the founding of the U.S. Federal Reserve in 1913 or when the U.S. took the dollar off the gold standard in 1971. Plus, there are both true stories and myths surrounding current price manipulations of gold and silver. Yes, there have certainly been times around the world when holding gold would have saved you from high inflation and devaluation if you timed it well, but these moments never arise suddenly. The U.S. dollar, the Euro, the Japanese Yen, and other currencies of countries with unsustainable levels of debt will all eventually be replaced—but when? You'll have plenty of warning for a currency devaluation to move your savings into a stronger currency or gold. Please have some perspective for the remaining 80% of the time when gold would not have helped or even hurt your financial situation. Never buy anything that you cannot afford—including a pile of shiny gold bars at the wrong time for an event that may not occur for quite some time.

FINANCIAL MECHANICS

Becoming aware of financial concepts does nothing to help you until you translate those concepts into rules and tasks that you actually follow in your life. These rules act as guardrails to keep you on track and out of financial trouble. If you have no rules for handling money, then I suspect that you probably have very little money compared to your income peers or keep experiencing avoidable financial problems. If you do not have proven money rules to follow, then you are left with emotions or ungrounded rules, neither of which will lead you to financial success. Money rules are personal choices that you employ to impose conceptual order on the physical money and assets that you control. These money rules guide your daily financial decisions. They are also mostly performed in private: no one knows if you have them, follow them, or how and when you change them. For example, everyone has heard the ancient money adage "save 10% of your income," and many people do this. In the absence of any other money rules, it is a fine place to start. How many money rules do you already know? Do you actually follow any of them? Do you know if your current rules are propelling you toward increasing financial stability or financial ruin? More importantly, how do you know for certain? Have you fully mapped them out or run them by an expert? From whom did you learn these rules—someone more likely to be broke or someone who has built substantial wealth and successfully taught others?

Next, what are your current money habits: where does your money normally end up each month? If you had to guess, what is your single biggest financial weakness or temptation? How would your friends answer this question about you? Are you willing to control this temptation or continually allow it to control you? Money rules and procedures will help guide you toward the best financial decisions so let's get started on them.

The most important and difficult question in all money management is, "What Can I Afford?" How, exactly, do you calculate this now? Write it out so you can compare it to what you'll learn in this section. One of the results of implementing this section is that you will be able to accurately determine what you can afford in as much detail as you would care to know.

The Four Money Routines

Managing the movement of money and values under your control requires you to develop four financial policies to guide your behavior:

1. Spending Routine
2. Saving Routine
3. Investing Routine
4. Oversight Routine

These four routines apply to individuals, households, non-profits, businesses, governments, or any other entity that seeks financial survival. Just so you are aware, the rules for the routines vary greatly depending upon the entity, and naturally, only personal routines will be discussed here.

Going through these routines, understanding them and completing them will give you the clarity you are seeking about your personal money matters. Some of these are time-consuming tasks but performing them is similar to brushing your teeth; you can either do them as a matter of course or face the predictable and unpleasant consequences.

These four routines also apply to anyone no matter what their age. I will go over them as simple rules for those under age 12, an intermediate level for teenagers, and then the full routines for adults who have started to earn money and are living on their own.

Routines for Children

These routines are simple for children age 12 and under, and should be done for them until they are old enough to do it for themselves, normally by 5–7 years old.

For children, the money that they receive is normally sporadic. Whenever they do receive any money from any source, half of the money is for them to spend and half of the money is to be set aside for investing (permanent wealth building).

This simple act does several things. First, it still allows the gratification of spending money while it builds the habit, at an early age, of allocating their income in a simple manner. As an adult, your money is going to be allocated in several categories and it will be solely up to you to defend these categories—from both yourself and others. The sooner they build the habit of setting aside money that will never be spent, the easier it will be for them to understand and follow through in setting aside savings for a short-term goal that they may want to purchase.

Here are the 4 routines for children:

1. Spending Routine = 50% of any income from any source is available to be spent on anything.
2. Savings Routine = no savings are mandatory. However, if the child wants to save up for a specific purchase, the money put into savings can only come from the Spending Routine money, not any other category of money.
3. Investing Routine = 50% of any income from any source must be placed in a separate location for permanent growth. This could be in short-term or long-term investments but this money can never be spent. The location for this money needs to be inaccessible to anyone but an adult. To start, it could be a jar, a safe, a simple savings account; but the adult must be the sentinel that prevents this money from being spent on anything. This money must be in a conceptual vault = money can go in but it can never be taken out, for any reason. Later, much later, some of its dividends or interest can be spent but that is far away for someone young.
4. Oversight Routine = a periodic review with the child of their growing net worth and where their money is invested, but they should have no physical control over this money until they have the maturity to do so.

Once a child reaches 5–7 years old, many parents also include an additional category for money to donate toward charitable giving or religious tithing. Offering a child a few choices and a percentage to donate accomplishes several psychological benefits. First, it puts them in a position of control when they are helpless to most of their world experience: they are directing where their personal effort will benefit, and in my experience it loosens the victim/tightwad/scarcity mentality that many people grow up around. If this is your choice as well, the rule for children is to take that percentage (3–10%) for donating and then the remaining amount of money is split evenly between spending and wealth building.

Routines for Teenagers

Once a child reaches age 13 they are capable of learning some budgeting basics, such as spending on clothes and school supplies for a semester. A parent's emotional capability to stick by the child's choice and not bail them out is how the children experience the results of their financial decisions. It is best for them to learn as many lessons as possible about money when they are young. This gives them the most practice when the stakes are low to make mistakes, plus they are building financial habits around sustainable money rules. Teaching your children nothing about money or the consequences of financial mismanagement has a very predictable and painful outcome in their future.

Depending on the maturity of the child, age 11–13 is also a time to prod them into earning some money for themselves: babysitting, dog walking, lawn service, tutoring or some other simple part-time service where they are creating money. If they desire gadgets, apparel, accessories, etc. (and what teenager doesn't?), they can now start to earn money to contribute for these items on their own. For example, after I was 12-years old, if there were something that I wanted buy, I had to contribute at least 50% of the price from my own savings. The details of those purchases have remained vivid in my memory. The more money that a child earns and controls responsibly, the more money that you would normally spend on them, you can now hand to them to manage on their own. If they are earning money, have them open a checking account and learn how to reconcile it each month; or open a low-balance credit card with you as the guarantor. Learning to handle these tools under your monthly supervision will give them a solid foundation that will keep them on track once they are on their own. As soon as a teenager has earned income, they are eligible to start putting some of those earnings in their own Roth IRA for tax-free growth for their retirement and getting them exposed to investing.

Routines for Adults

After high school or college, and you begin living on your own with a career or job, it is time to advance and become aware of the full financial routines. Now, it is highly unlikely that you will have many of these to address at first, but any of them could be appropriate to your circumstances, so here is the entire agenda.

I. Spending Routine:

Step 1. Create spending targets: ratios and dollar amounts.
To begin, you need to create a master spending schedule. This is a list of categories where you spend your money. A spending schedule of the past is helpful but not nearly as important as where you are going to direct your money in the future. This list should only be as detailed as you need it to be. As an example, you could have a category called grocery shopping. If there is a question in this area in the future, you can break it down further into subcategories such as cleaning supplies, snacks, meat, alcohol, or whatever to highlight any question that you have in mind. I advise only using categories that are easy to collect instead of starting with an endless schedule with details to the nth-degree that will not aid in decision-making. This is because you will not start, let alone continue, itemizing these if it is too difficult, cumbersome, time-consuming or unhelpful.

Once you have your spending schedule, you need to determine your personal spending targets for critical ratios. Before I discuss these ratios, understand that there are many places where you can find "average expenses." These reference points are worse than useless because most people have no idea what they are doing with their money, let alone being on track for financial success over their lifetime. You should not care what the average person is doing in any area, let alone money management. If you use average numbers or ratios, you will be following the herd into financial struggle.

Next, there are critical ratios that I call the **Four Horsemen of Financial Ratios;** violate them at your financial peril. These are ratios based on your after-tax income; the net amount of earnings that you receive that is available for spending. These four ratios make up the bulk of your fixed expenses that help to reveal what is available for your variable spending each month. The first ratio of the four horsemen happens to be in the spending category (the other three are discussed later) and it is a housing ratio maximum of 25%. Your housing expense is calculated by your rent plus renter's insurance or your mortgage (minus the interest tax credit), plus property taxes, homeowner's insurance and any other association fees.

This is the first and most important ratio for you to target because where you live determines many other aspects of your lifestyle spending. When you violate this housing ratio by spending more than 25%, then some part of your life will become underfunded. It will show up in some part of your life such as not having enough money for normal repairs, clothing, children, insurance, etc., and most significantly, your retirement. Many readers may know that mortgage guidelines allow this ratio to be far higher at 36%, so why is the number presented here so much more conservative? Mortgage guidelines are only designed to protect banks from foreclosure and not to lead you toward financial success. I do not recommend living anywhere near 36% unless your career is on track for a sharply increasing income. Your housing ratio is also important because where you live greatly influences many aspects of your spending. It influences who your friends are, the type of furnishings you buy, the vacations you take, the cars you consider to buy, the toys your children will be hounding you about, your clothing, landscaping, gadgets, appliances, restaurants, home updates, etc. The accumulation of all these influences will either create an environment that supports appropriate spending for your income or tempts you to match some of their spending or activities that may be unaffordable to your income. It only takes a single temptation on a continual basis to bust your budgeting. I have seen this pattern play out over and over again, regardless of income, education, or age. Someone buys more house than they can afford, putting them in contact with neighbors and friends with a lot more disposable income, then they start spending beyond their means until some under-funded area of their life turns into a financial crisis. Then they call me wondering how it all happened and can I magically fix it for them.

What about owning a second home? There is no special exemption for your housing situation. No matter how many homes you are planning to buy, for them to be affordable to your income the combined expense from all of them must remain below 25% of your income.

Your housing ratio is the only ratio that I recommend keeping an eye on for your consumption. In my experience, the more rigidly you structure the rest of your spending ratios (food, entertainment, gasoline, etc.), the less accurate and meaningful it will become to your particular lifestyle. For example, someone single who is living downtown in a large city without a vehicle will have incomparable ratios to a family living in a small town with a different mix of living expenses. Instead of using ratios, however, you still need to fill out a spending schedule from your current expenses to analyze where you stand, where to make important trade-offs once you later fill out your saving and investing schedules.

Monthly Spending Schedule Example:

After-Tax Income . . . . $_____
Housing . . . . $_____
Utilities. . . . . $_____
Insurance . . . . $_____
Entertainment, Gifts, Vacations. . . . . $_____
Clothing, Shoes. . . . . $_____
Repairs, Maintenance . . . . $_____
Transportation. . . . . $_____
Savings. . . . . $_____
Investing. . . . . $_____
Other. . . . . $_____

The reason you must complete a spending schedule is because this is the only way to determine if, when, and where you are overspending or to isolate spending anomalies that need to be addressed.

It is up to you to decide what level of detailed breakdown of your spending is necessary for you to personally understand what is going on with your money. How do you know what level of detail is needed? If you can determine from your spending schedule last month and this month whether your spending is on target for your current month (along with additions to savings and investing), then you have done enough. If you do not know why an expense is going up or down, then you need to split your spending into more detailed categories. For example, I normally do not track food as a separate item in my spending schedule; it is lumped with credit card charges each month. But there have been a few times that I had to separate food categories into: restaurants and different kinds of grocery stores to determine where there was a mysterious increase in spending that I wanted to discover and reduce. A few people track this level of detailed spending all the time, but your decision should be based on what level of effort and detail works for you and your family as an ongoing routine. The categories and sub-categories for spending are endless. You need to determine from several months of your past spending which ones are relevant to you over the next 12 months. Some of your categories will also change over time.

Most people track money in the time period of their paycheck: weekly, biweekly, or monthly. The time period you should use is whatever works for you; there are some people who have a daily amount of money to spend. Some calculate all of their fixed costs so that each day they have X amount of variable spending, whether it is clothing, food, or whatever. If you find yourself too far off track at the end of the quarter or month, then perhaps you should shorten up to weekly or daily to determine where your overspending is occurring.

For example, while I was driving errands with my wife she asked me if I wanted to go out for dinner. I replied, "Sure, but you know we cannot afford it this week." She replied, "Certainly grown adults can afford one dinner!," because it seemed ridiculous to her that I took our spending rules so seriously. We both knew that we had already spent our entire variable spending earlier that day. So even with the financial stability that we have, the rules of our money management came first over a meal at a restaurant. Although it was a small expense, conceptually, it would have been borrowing tomorrow's food, living above our means, etc.—and that is absolutely forbidden. I have seen the tragic end of that storyline in others' lives too many times to start that bad habit.

Is all budgeting about minimizing your life with financial constraints? In my view it is liberating to finally be aware of your current financial reality. It is the primary step toward prioritizing what is important to you in your life so that you can make sure you have the funds to support those goals. By highlighting and reducing costs on items that are not important, you then have more money to spend on things that are important you; the things that add the most to your life. Each item on your spending list is something that you are financially supporting. Your spending schedule allows you to scrutinize for trade-offs in an ongoing manner. This is even more important for a family with many members and divergent desires.

By using your spending schedule, you can adjust your behavior to make certain your goals, priorities, values, passions, and ideas are financially supported. Without this simple tool, you are guessing that you are doing the right things but you do not really know if you are in a financially stable position.

Once you have split your money into categories, then you must defend those categories: you do not steal from your retirement assets to buy a car, or steal from your children's college savings account to pay for a vacation. You are the only sentinel to defend your financial priorities from being consumed when it is expedient. How do you do this? Whenever you want to take money from one category to spend in another—think about what you would do if you did not have any money? You would pretend you are in high school and grab some quick money by cutting grass, cleaning gutters, organizing clutter, freelance projects online, or even get a part-time job. Defend your categories of money from other people and yourself, or you will eventually find a way to justify any spending until your important goals and values will be left unfunded.

Step 2. Check your actual spending amounts and ratios each month. Each category on your spending schedule needs to balance to your income. In order to maintain this balance, each category will have a target dollar amount. In the short-term, you have fixed expenses that you cannot change. The remainder of your spending is described as variable that you can choose to increase or eliminate. (In the long-term, all of your spending is variable; if you so choose.)

Step 3. Forecast your cash-flow requirements each month for the next 12 months to determine if you have enough income.

Look at your past spending as the basis from which you forecast all of your future cash-flow needs. From this, perhaps for the first time you are managing your financial life 12 months into the future. So you will have plenty of time to take action and change your behavior to handle money problems long before they arise. Some bills arrive quarterly, annually, or sporadically and you do not want to be caught short on cash when they arrive. This should not happen to you again as the more thoroughly you forecast your cash-flow schedule, the more accurately you can plan for many types of financial scenarios that may play out.

One simple way to minimize cash-flow planning is to maintain one extra month's expenses in your checking account. This way you can pay every normal bill the moment it arrives, knowing that you have the money to cover it. Or, in months that there is extra money, it can be transferred into a savings account to earn some interest before it is transferred back during the month that it is required.

You can move further into your future planning by thinking about your expectations over the next 5 years. Do you have any planned trips, changes in transportation needs, new children or living situation changes, large purchases, expected raises, Washington talking about tax changes, etc.? Anything that may change in your life may impact your financial schedules. Planning for all of these as early as possible is how you will adjust and move more seamlessly with events as they unfold.

Step 4. Seek to reduce large expenses or improve income sources. The marketplace is always changing, so once a year spend a little effort to see if you can reduce some of your utilities and large expenses. I have never had a company call me to let me know they are reducing their prices; it is solely up to you to make sure that you are not over-paying. Improving income sources is paramount to financial success: investments, side income, career advancement, business ownership, etc. All of these are large subjects unto themselves, but again, once a year you should be proactive in making improvements in these areas.

After your review, you can determine where and how much to make adjustments in your spending behavior. You are the only one who can maintain your spending on its targets. The easiest way to address this is to comparison shop and make trade-offs. If your housing is too high, move to lower your rent, refinance your mortgage, change your insurance company, rent out the garage or a room, etc. The more ambitious way to solve spending overages is to create more income, but beware that if you are unable to manage your smaller income, you may not manage a higher income much better.

Step 5. Cycle back to Step-1 once a year. You can do these steps as periodically as you want. But normally, enough will have changed in any given year that it will be worthwhile to go back through these steps to make sure your spending schedule is all-inclusive, expenses are contained, additions to savings and investments are on track, and your financial forecasts go out several years so that you are not caught short on money.

II. Savings Routine:

Before any discussion on savings, it must be defined. When you hear "save 10% of your money" what exactly does that mean? If I have $1,000 in savings, when can it be spent? On what? The definition of savings for this book = a reserve of money that has:

1. A specific purpose
2. An estimated dollar amount
3. An expected date to be spent

Savings is not investing or investments, although it may be placed into some type of a safe investment for a return. Let's start with an example. In 6 months I want to take my family of 4 on a vacation. I now have the purpose, the date, and I have an expected amount that this particular vacation will cost around $3,600. So now I can start a savings schedule for this vacation. Starting with $0 today, I need to set aside $600 each month ($3,600 divided by 6) for the next 6 months so that I will have the full amount to pay for this vacation when it occurs. Each month I need to verify that there has been an additional $600 set aside in savings identified for this vacation. Otherwise our vacation will not be fully funded and we will either have to forego this vacation or borrow the money, which you already know is forbidden.

Conceptually, your savings schedule is similar to an

irrigation system. Inflows of money are being split among all of your crops to nourish them so that they can grow to maturity when you can harvest them. If you fail to set aside adequate savings, your goals will wither, be postponed, and possibly may perish. These goals actually represent your personal values and passions, and if you want to express them you must fully fund them at some point. Now, there are many goals that require no money but they may require something else from you: time, effort, training, practice, etc. But to the extent that money is also required, your savings schedule is the tool to map out what you need to do to make certain that they will be realized on time.

Step 1. Create a master savings schedule of financial goals that you want to achieve within several years including all of the maintenance and replacement of items that you already own.

Write down the description along with the expected dollar amount and expected date. Then divide that dollar amount by the number of months until your target date. The result is the amount of money that you need to set aside into savings each month to reach this goal.

Aside from your list of savings goals, I am going to give you four mandatory goals to be included on your savings schedule.

First is an emergency fund. This is money whose sole purpose is a reserve to bridge your expenses when you are between jobs. If your income stops, how many months does it normally take someone in your profession or your area to find a new one? This is the minimum number of months that your expenses need to be covered in case your income stops, for whatever reason. This money must be set aside in some form so that it can be immediately available for spending. Some people are comfortable if they have enough money set aside to cover 3 months of expenses while others insist on 12 months; but base your monthly target off of your expectation of how long you may potentially be without an income. If you currently do not have an emergency fund this may appear to be a daunting dollar amount in light of other goals that you have. Just chip away by contributing each month toward this fund. This emergency fund is not to be spent on unexpected repairs or one-time expenses; that money must come from some other savings fund that you have. It is solely up to you to defend your categories of money and if you have an employment or income gap you will be very relieved that you followed this hard-learned advice. Life is unpredictable and many people mistakenly spend down their emergency fund on chronic problems. If you do this a few times, your emergency fund will be dangerously underfunded or nonexistent. You should also have an "Unexpected Expense" fund for things like a medical emergency, a critical car or home repair, etc., but the money should not come from your emergency fund; again, that is designated solely for a loss of your earned income.

The **second** mandatory savings goal is a minimum of 5% of your after-tax income for maintenance and repairs. Having money available for expected repairs and maintenance is so important that this rule is the 2nd of the Four Horsemen of Financial Ratios. This 5% number is just an estimate that works in many scenarios. But as soon as you can, build a savings schedule like the one below in this section to create the most accurate number to your personal circumstances. To do this you will need to make a list of all the items in your life that you are responsible for repairing and replacing.

The **third** mandatory savings goal is a minimum of 6% of your after-tax income for your next vehicle. Outside of a city-walking distance lifestyle, transportation is a major ongoing expense and managing this expense is so important that it is the 3rd of the Four Horsemen of Financial Ratios. This money is not for current car payments nor is it for repairs and maintenance for your current vehicle; this savings is solely for the purchase outlay of your next vehicle.

While you are using your current vehicle, you need to be saving up for your next vehicle. Your current vehicle is dropping in value each year as it is consumed by time and usage. This loss in value must be offset by adding a similar amount of money to a reserve for your next vehicle or you are depleting your transportation assets. If you fail to make this reserve, then you will be will stuck with needlessly expensive options to fund your replacement vehicle, either borrowing or leasing.

When you need or want to get a new vehicle you just check the amount that you have accumulated in this fund to see how much you can spend on your next vehicle purchase. If it is only $3,000, then that is the maximum that you can spend on your new vehicle. This $3,000 is not for a down payment for a lease or a loan. If you want to be extra-financially prudent, then whatever vehicle you purchase would also be at least two years old with low miles. Why the 6% number? When you save less than this percentage your new car fund may not accumulate large enough by the time your current vehicle needs to be replaced. If you save a lot more than this percentage then you may be financially starving some other area of your life. Like all spending estimates, as soon as you finish mapping out your savings schedule with your personal details, you should replace this 6% vehicle rule because you'll have a more accurate number for your particular circumstances.

The **fourth** mandatory savings goal is to work toward owning a home without any mortgage before any potential retirement date. The housing expense of a mortgage or rent is one of your largest ongoing expenses. If someone approaching retirement still has a mortgage or rent payments, then it dramatically reduces the likelihood that they will be able to successfully retire. Some retirees have a "failed retirement" where they reach retirement age and quit but then are forced to return to work within a few years to make ends meet. Even though no housing payment prior to retirement is the goal, there are two ways to get there: 1) Owning a home with no mortgage or 2) Having a rental reserve to make rent payments. But both methods involve monthly payments, either to your banker through your mortgage or to yourself into a rental reserve. When you have an amortizing mortgage, part of your mortgage payment pays down the balance of the loan each month. But you do not have to own a home (you could rent your whole life), but in this case it is up to you to self-fund your own housing fund for your retirement years. The purpose of this housing fund is to fully-fund your rent payments during your retirement. The amount of money that you need to set aside for either a down payment for a home that you plan to buy or your retirement housing fund is = at least 20% of your current rent payment.

Remember that your housing should not exceed 25% of your after-tax income so you could use the calculation of 5% of your income (your housing ratio of 25% multiplied by your retirement rental reserve of 20%) of your income to put toward a retirement housing reserve. So whether you build your own housing reserve for renting or have a mortgage that is amortizing the balance down, either way you are building your net worth at a similar rate.

Savings Schedule Example—For a Homeowner:

	Expected Lifespan	Current Age	Expected Cost	Current Accrual	Cost Per Yr	Cost Per Mth	Percentage End Life
Emergency Fund			18,000	18,000			
New Car	10	4	22,000	8,800	2,200	183	40%
Air-conditioner	20	11	4,000	2,200	200	17	55%
Furnace	20	11	4,000	2,200	200	17	55%
Carpeting	8	4	4,000	2,000	500	42	50%
Paint Interior	8	5	3,000	1,875	375	31	63%
Paint Exterior	8	2	4,000	1,000	500	42	25%
Furniture	15	11	7,500	5,500	500	42	73%
Driveway	20	11	3,500	1,925	175	15	55%
Windows	20	11	2,500	1,375	125	10	55%
Roof	30	11	7,500	2,750	250	21	37%
Computer/TV	8	3	2,500	938	313	26	38%
Total			**$ 82,500**	**$ 48,563**	**$ 5,338**	**$ 445**	

This schedule requires the expected lifespan of your significant assets that need to be replaced, the current age, and the expected cost of the replacement or treatment. Simple math will reveal how much money you need to set aside each month, each year, and how much money you currently must have set aside to replace these assets.

Expected Lifespan = how many years you expect the item to last

Current Age = how many years old the item is today

Expected cost = your expected total cost to replace this item

Current Accrual = how much money you should have already set aside today to replace the item, formula: Expected Cost times (Current Age divided by Expected Lifespan)

Cost per Year = Expected Cost divided by the Expected Lifespan

Cost per Month = Cost per Year divided by 12, the amount of money you should be putting into a savings account each month.

Note that in this example, you need to be setting aside $445 each month in order to fund your list of replacements once they come to the end of their useful life. If your savings accrual is under-funded, you will need to add additional money to this $445 to get back on track.

Step 2. Calculate your monthly savings contributions to compare their trajectory to your list of targeted amounts and dates. Financial calculators can determine how much interest you will earn based on the rate on the savings account that you have chosen. Once you have your schedule setup, you need to periodically determine if you are still on track to fund these goals. The sooner you are aware of a shortfall, the sooner you can re-assess what you are working toward and what changes you may need to make to get there.

Step 3. Seek new savings vehicles. There are a few reasons that you want to periodically review where you are holding your savings. There are minimum balances for certain types of accounts that you may have surpassed, changes in interest rates, new competitors, and changes in the marketplace. Your money must be working as hard as you are to contribute to your financial goals. When interest rates are low the tiny interest earned on your savings will be frustrating. But when interest rates are relatively high, the interest income alone can materially contribute to your savings goals. Your savings can be held in different forms or accounts as your balance grows, but you should be taking very little or no risk with this money so that it is available when you plan to spend the money.

Step 4. Cycle back to Step-1 once a year. Just like your spending schedule, in a year there can be many changes in your circumstances and goals that need to be reflected in your savings schedule as well.

Some people have never saved money in their lives. When anyone starts to look at their savings and investing schedules, it can be a bit of a shock to learn how far above your means that you were spending. So there may be a rough transition period to change some of your ingrained spending habits to allow you proper savings and investing contributions.

I understand how difficult it seems when you do not feel that you are living extravagantly but then determine for yourself that you will have to cut some spending to meet your savings goals. From working with many people, here is a temporary transition plan: pick a percentage that is no lower than 3% and no higher than 10% to set aside from any and all income that you receive into a separate savings account. If you start with more than 10% it is too much of a leap. When people start from zero and start saving over 10% before you have had a chance to lower your fixed expenses, it becomes too painful, they quickly abandon the whole idea, and never make it a habit to save anything. Also, if you start saving with a number under 3%, then your new account will be so tiny that you will feel that it is not even worth the effort and abandon the idea within a few months as well. When many of your spending habits are unaffordable it can be a slow and difficult adjustment to make. Seeing your financial schedules highlight your financial issues is not enough, you must change your behavior and this 3–10% savings assignment has been a proven temporary-stepping stone for many people until you get your financial life on stable footing. As you adjust your fixed costs and thoroughly map out your savings schedule, you can move away from the 3–10% training-wheels to your true savings needs from your detailed savings schedule.

III. Investing Routine:

Step 1. Create a master investing schedule, similar to your savings schedule, for financial goals that will take more than five years to accumulate from your contributions and its earnings.

This list is generated by determining all of the long-term purposes that you have for accumulating money and assets. For example, buying a home, a wedding, replacing a salary for one parent to stay home, college funds, retirement, a significant charitable gift, or building a legacy of financial opportunity for heirs.

Aside from your personal list of investing goals there is one mandatory goal that everyone must have on their investing schedule. This rule is so important that it is the 4th of the Four Horsemen of Financial Ratios. The rule is to contribute 15%

of your income toward your retirement. It does not matter if this 15% is before-tax for pre-tax retirement accounts or after-tax to be put into post-tax accounts, but the minimum amount must be at least 15% of your income from any source.[27,28,29] Research on retirement lifestyles based on savings rates during employment found that:

- People who put only 10% or less of their income into retirement accounts struggled financially during their retirement.

- People who saved 20% or more of their income were able to increase their lifestyle spending compared to their working career.

In order for you to avoid being both poor and too old to work, I highly recommend that you start with a target of 15%. If you have not been doing this up to now, start making up for lost time by increasing this percentage to catch-up your retirement funding.

Although this 15% is a one-size-fits-all starting point, I urge you to determine if this number is too high or too low for your particular situation. You will need to gather some information in order to use retirement calculators that will most accurately assess how much you need to save for retirement. These factors are: your age, your expected retirement age, your life expectancy, your current retirement savings amount, your retirement income needs, pension income, and your expected savings rate. If you are just starting your work career, these numbers are wild guesses, but at least start with a 15% savings rate so you have the best chance at reaching your retirement target.

Each goal on your investment schedule will have a withdrawal date in the future, either a single or series of dates indicating when you are going to spend the money. Once your targeted date is less than 5 years, then you should take it off your investing schedule and move it to your savings schedule. This is because it is imprudent to keep these funds at risk where the price volatility of your investments may fall and not give you enough time to recover before you need to spend the money. Please do not take the risk being unable to afford your goal once you are within 5 years of your target date. After every stock market downturn there are articles written about people who planned on imminently retiring who now have to work for many more years to recover their risky stock-market losses. When you are setting aside money for investing, you cannot choose where to place it until you first determine when it will be spent. Scheduling the date that this money needs to be available in spendable cash determines where and how it can be invested.

Be aware that the more money you have under your control then the financial consequences of your decisions become much bigger. Becoming more financially literate and mapping out your options is always the best way to keep improving your financial stability.

Investing Schedule Example—Family with Two Children:

	Initial Years	Remaining Years	Funding Target	Current Value	Addition Per Year	Addition Per Month
Family Reunion	6	5	7,500	1,137	1,116	93
College #1	18	9	100,000	52,455	3,804	317
College #2	18	13	100,000	21,017	3,804	317
Retirement	42	33	1,200,000	119,232	11,028	919
Total			$ 1,407,500	$ 193,841	$ 19,752	$ 1,646

Step 2. Compute the contributions necessary to reach your investing targets based on your expected investing returns. Financial calculators will figure out your monthly or annual contributions but first there is one variable you need to determine: what return you may reasonably expect to achieve.

If you have an investing track record then you can use your historical return rate. If you are investing in a particular bond that will mature when you need the money, use the yield on that bond. Otherwise, if you are investing in a portfolio of stocks and bonds, I would recommend using 4% as your expected average investment return rate. I have never come across a financial study that shows the average investor earning an annualized rate much over 4% for a period of 20 years or longer. This is a realistic and conservative number for your investment return because it is far more prudent to potentially overshoot your financial targets than to come up short when you need the money. Again, once you have an actual investing track record you can use this as your more accurate expected return rate.

Just like your savings schedule, you can now map out the trajectory of contributions you'll need to reach your investing targets.

Step 3. Create your own investing rules for your investments based on your current investing capability. This is based on your interest, knowledge, time, experience, and resources. You can start immediately by using the Allocate and Rebalance Portfolio that you already learned in Section 3.

Some other investing rules that you might consider:

- Only invest in stocks that have increased their dividends each year for the last 20 years and are trading in the bottom quarter of the 5-year price range.
- Only invest in rental real estate near universities for stable demand.
- Only use an investment operator who provides you with an audited 5-year track record.

Whatever investing vehicles you have chosen, you need to be knowledgeable enough to build rules around them. These rules aid in increasing the likelihood of success, minimizing losses, and increasing the robustness of earning a favorable return on your money.

Let's go through an example: You want to fully fund a college education for a 5-year-old child. Your estimate is that it will roughly cost $100,000 starting in 13 years. Find an online financial calculator and using a 4% expected return rate, you determine that this will require contributions of $490 per month over the next 13 years. If you can earn a better return, you will have extra money or you can lower the monthly contributions later on.

College Savings Account Forecast Example:

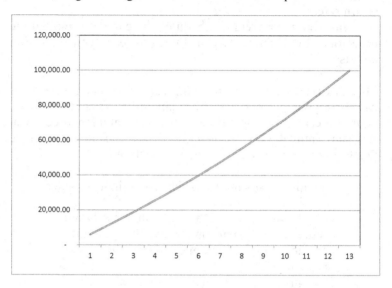

Step 4. Seek new investment strategies, tactics, individual investments, advisors, and money managers. The world of investing is always in flux and even if you are doing something simple like the Allocate and Rebalance Portfolio method, then there may be some opportunity for you to find a better way to lower your risk and increase your return for your investing money.

Step 5. Measure and compare your actual investment results to appropriate stock and bond indexes to your investing schedule. Your investments are going to fluctuate in value and it is important to highlight if the strategy you have selected is keeping up or falling behind. If your strategy is consistently falling behind, then it may be time to adjust your strategy, your particular investments, or your contributions to make certain that you will reach your goals.

Step 6. Cycle back to Step-1 at least once per year to re-assess your targets and investments. The investing world continually changes with new products, new theories, and of course a changing economic landscape. Your investing goals may have also changed during the year. For these reasons, it is important to go through these steps at least once a year to make sure your investing plan is still on track for your goals.

IV. Oversight Routine:

Step 1. Calculate your net worth (assets minus debts) to analyze its components for optimal growth. The only way to know you are optimizing your finances is to complete a net worth schedule along with the interest rates you are receiving and paying.

Net Worth Statement Example:

ASSETS			LIABILITIES		NET WORTH	
Checking Account	$	2,831	Credit Cards	$ 663	$	2,168
Savings Acct 1.00%		4,180				4,180
Savings Acct 1.05%		37,218				37,218
Liquid Assets:	$	44,229		$ 663	$	43,566
Roth IRA		4,563				4,563
Roth IRA		5,982				5,982
401(k)		43,386				43,386
Qualified Accounts:	$	53,931		$ -	$	53,931
Car		12,850				12,850
Vehicles:	$	12,850		$ -	$	12,850
Home		85,000	Mortgage 4.375%	58,650		26,350
Rental Home		65,000	Mortgage 5.125%	45,500		19,500
Real Estate:	$	150,000		$ 104,150	$	45,850
Brokerage Account		16,744				16,744
College Fund		41,907				41,907
Inflation Bonds		2,614				2,614
Other Investments:	$	61,265		$ -	$	61,265
Total Assets:	$	322,275	Total Liabilities:	$ 104,813 Net Worth	$	217,462

Step 2. Monitor, maintain, and improve your assets; both financial and physical. Your net worth statement serves as a periodic financial report card to reveal where you are improving or degrading your financial condition and to examine if you are on track for meeting your financial goals. For example: If you have debts, are they declining as you expected each month as you pay down on the principal balance? Can you get lower interest rates on any of your loans? Are your productive assets increasing in value? Are you adding to your productive assets

each month? Are you maintaining your physical assets (car, home, boat, furnishings, etc.) or letting them unnecessarily erode in value?

As a financial tool, filling out a periodic balance sheet brings reality to your attention so you can attend to problems before they get worse, increase your awareness as you make financial decisions, and highlight improvements that you can make. Moving around your debt and equity is something that I review a few times a year as components change. For example, interest rates you are paying and receiving change and sometimes thresholds are reached where moving money is more beneficial for your situation. A simple example is paying off a very-high interest rate loan by having access to a very-low interest rate somewhere else. An increase in your tax rate may prompt you to move money into a tax-free investment. As your financial stability increases so will the number of components on your balance sheet and your net worth statement is the only way to examine all of them at once.

You can employ any manner of schedules that aid in your financial decision-making. Your personal financial statements serve as tools to highlight your financial issues and progress. If you are not sure where to begin, any tracking would be helpful if it supports the platitude, "It does not matter how much money much you make. What matters is how much you keep and how hard that works for you." Your financial statements will reveal where there are opportunities to increase "how much you keep" and ratcheting up how much that money is earning. Examine your schedules in any way you find helpful – using ratios, adding additional categories or lumping others together, any facet to clarify what is a problem or what is an opportunity.

Other Financial Schedules:

Financial Drivers - monthly
It doesn't matter how much you make; 1) how much you keep and 2) how hard it works for you.

	Jan	Feb	Mar	Apr	May	Jun
Additions To Accounts						
Roth IRA	50	50	50	50	50	50
Roth IRA	50	50	50	50	50	50
Investment Accounts	150	175	-	150	150	150
Savings Reserve	180	180	180	180	180	180
401(k)	150	150	150	150	150	150
Sub-Total	580	605	430	580	580	580
Debt - Reduction of Principal						
Home Mortgage	45	45	46	46	47	47
Rental Mortgage	38	38	38	38	39	39
Student Loan	80	80	80	80	80	80
Sub-Total	163	163	164	164	166	166
Additions To Net Worth	**743**	**768**	**594**	**744**	**746**	**746**
% of Income	25%	26%	20%	25%	25%	25%
Net Investment Income						
Interest on Savings Accounts	3	4	4	3	3	4
Brokerage Account	58	31	35	57	31	35
Rental Home	17	128	128	53	128	78
Roth IRA	31	19	23	31	19	23
Roth IRA	31	19	23	31	19	23
401(k)	113	80	78	113	80	78
Sub-Total	253	281	291	288	280	241
% on Net Productive Assets	0.2%	0.2%	0.2%	0.2%	0.2%	0.2%
Realized Capital Gains						
Retirement Account Trades	196		30	(181)		421
Real Estate						
Other			(218)		75	
Sub-Total	196	-	(188)	(181)	75	421
Total Investment Cash Flow	**449**	**281**	**103**	**107**	**355**	**662**
Unrealized Capital Gains						
Roth IRA	342	121	(60)	(39)	14	(108)
Roth IRA	342	121	(60)	(39)	14	(108)
IRA	1,071	492	(279)	(123)	83	(680)
Other						
Sub-Total	1,755	734	(399)	(201)	111	(896)
% on Net Productive Assets	1.50%	0.63%	-0.34%	-0.17%	0.09%	-0.77%
Total Investment Gains/Losses	**2,204**	**1,015**	**(296)**	**(94)**	**466**	**(234)**
% on Net Productive Assets	1.9%	0.9%	-0.3%	-0.1%	0.4%	-0.2%
Benchmark S&P 500 Index	4.5%	4.3%	3.3%	0.0%	-6.0%	1.6%
Average Productive Assets	117,000	117,000	117,000	117,000	117,000	117,000
Cash Income	3,000	3,000	3,000	3,000	3,000	3,000

Step 3. Periodic review of your credit rating for errors and improvement. Your personal credit rating not only affects your ability to get credit and what interest rates you will pay, but it also impacts your insurance rates and sometimes your ability to be hired. For whatever is going on in your life, or what future uses there may be for credit ratings, you have the most options and cheapest options if you maintain a high credit score. Credit scores are calculated by ratings agencies and how they are calculated is a trade secret, but there are some generally recognized factors. These are: on-time payment counts for 35% of the score (keep a month's expenses in your checking account to minimize the stress of making sure you have enough money for bills); outstanding credit card balances at less than 25% of their maximum level account for 30% of the score; the length of time an account has been open is 15% of the score (the longer, the better); and having different types of debt is another 10% of the score.

By reviewing your credit score once a year, you can clear off any mistakes that have been made (these happen to most everyone) so that when you need credit there will not be any delays while you scramble to fix years of errors. If you have a damaged credit score based on your past history, there are many free sources of information about the tactics to improve it as quickly as possible.

Step 4. Periodic insurance review for changes in circumstances and needs. Changes in your personal circumstances frequently require a corresponding change in your insurance needs. Staying on top of this is important so that you are not missing: changes by the insurance company; wasting money by being over-insured, or worse, being underinsured when a problem occurs. You may also want to re-examine the possibility of self-insurance for certain items, as mentioned earlier.

Step 5. Periodic estate planning and asset protection review for changes in law and circumstances; along with a review of your legal entities. Changes in your personal circumstances can require a corresponding change in your estate planning needs. Additionally, changes in state and federal rules each year may prompt a change for your estate planning or the entities that you control (company, trust, partnership, etc.) even though your personal situation has not changed. Staying on top of this is important so your wishes are up to date, legally current, and legal entities are still optimal for your situation.

Step 6. Periodic meeting with financial and legal advisors. Many people have a Will and simple taxes, so spending money on advisors may not be needed. If you are financially ambitious, it is likely that sooner or later your financial life may require more support from experts. Just owning a rental property or a side business opens up a whole new world of legal and tax consequences. For these two examples, while you have to perform more paperwork you can also take advantage of tax deductions and tax benefits that are unavailable to employees. Your team may include a lawyer, tax attorney, accountant, bookkeeper, legal entity specialist, financial advisor, investment advisor, trustees, banker, and others. It is up to you to find and hire the talent that you need and then coordinate with them so your financial life is a unified plan for your optimal benefit.

Step 7. Periodic advisor review for coaching or replacement. When advisors are not meeting your needs, let them know immediately. These situations may occur because of a misunderstanding that needs to be clarified, a change in your expectations from them, or they may not be able to meet your needs, for whatever reason. As your needs change, you may also need to change advisors to someone that addresses them better. I had a business tax specialist for a long time but he knew little about real estate, so I had to replace him when I started to buy investment real estate. You need to assess what is going on to know if you need to give them more accurate feedback or if it is time to replace them with someone else more appropriate for what you are planning to do over the next several years.

Step 8. Cycle back to Step-1, once per year. As with all of the four routines (spending, saving, investing, oversight), there may be enough changes in your life that you should perform all of these steps at least once a year to make sure that you are addressing everything you need to around your financial life.

Putting All 4 Routines Together

It is my experience that whenever one or more of these oversight tasks has been repeatedly overlooked, then your net worth is far smaller than what it could have been; plus you are likely to be unknowingly dancing in a mine-field of financial risk.

Once you have completed these four routines, you are finally in a position to calculate the answer to that all-important question that you use every day: "Can I afford this purchase"?

- Do you have your Savings Schedule filled out?
- Do you have your Investing Schedule filled out?
- Is there enough money available in your Spending Schedule to support all of the savings and investing contributions that you calculated?
- Do you know what variable spending is available to you each month?

If these schedules do not balance out yet, then you have some priorities to work out until they do. To increase spending in one area you must cut back in others that are not as important to you; or find a way to make more money.

Be aware that no matter how high your level of income may become, there is no amount of money that cannot be outspent. Every year there are high income athletes, entertainers, and lottery winners who file for bankruptcy because they never learned the financial literacy in this book. In contrast, I had a breakfast meeting with someone who had become financially successful from a lifetime of high financial literacy and business literacy. Although he had started with nothing, his net worth was now a tremendous number. During this breakfast at an expensive hotel he complained that the hotel wanted to charge $5 to clean socks; he said, "That's ridiculous, a few washings would cost more than a new pair of socks so I just wash them in the sink myself." Behind all of his financial success was still a long-standing habit of comparison shopping, frugal evaluation, and setting priorities on where he wanted to spend money and save money.

The combination of all of your financial schedules clarifies exactly where you are and what you must do to support your life, your dreams, your values, and your future. These schedules are not just a few numbers to look over and file away; they are your financial tools to craft your life:

1. Your Spending Schedule is your microscope to measure, isolate, and diagnose financial variances and problems.
2. Your Cash Flow Schedule is your telescope to navigate your financial life over the next 12 months to several years.
3. Your Saving and Investing Schedules are your irrigation systems to allocate enough money to support your personal goals.
4. Your Oversight Routine is your scanning procedure to evaluate your overall financial life and detect any structural problems.

If you have not completed the four routines of money management, begin them now. Some people like to start with pencil and paper, while others prefer spreadsheets or smartphone apps, plus many banks offer free online tools or software. Choose whatever mix of tools is most suitable to you in accomplishing *all* of your schedules and financial tasks. You will learn best by putting together any tools yourself, personalizing them, and then refining them as they become part of your regular household tasks. (My father has always done all of this in his head, so it wasn't obvious to me that he was doing anything!) The first time you go through these routines, it is by far the most difficult. After that, much of the work is simply fine tuning or an easy annual task. Once you begin the habit of completing these routines, many people keep them up because they now know that they are flying blind without them. Completing these routines is not only the starting point to manage your financial life, it is also a test. If you are unable to get these done, in my opinion, you are not yet capable enough to purchase a home, investment real estate, start or buy a business, or manage budgets for your employer. Completing these routines *is* the financial foundation that all of your financial advancements will be built upon. The more thoroughly you embrace all of these routines, the more financial stability and personal goals you will be able to accomplish over your lifetime.

Conclusion

Congratulations: you have made your way through information that, when fully implemented, will provide you with all of the clarity you need for successful financial decision making. You will have more financial control over the drama of life, experience less financial stress, and be more able to financially support your dreams. Any implementation of these ideas is going to improve your financial stability and give you a more solid base for how financially ambitious you would like to become.

You have a table to review the weak vs. strong handed-traits to discover where your behavior may need to change to improve your financial condition. The more you go over these traits, the more clarity you will have about your attitude in different areas and where you may want to make some progress.

Now that you are also alert for needless opportunity costs, you know that the faster you act, the fewer opportunity costs are accruing around you. Over time, as you follow the four routines, you will be incurring far fewer of these opportunity costs.

Continue to use this book as a reference as some items you may have glossed over, or perhaps changes in your circumstances will offer new challenges that you had not considered at your first read. When you are confronted with a new situation or potential money rule, first review the 15 concepts in this book. Your decisions should be in alignment with these 15 concepts and an enhancement of them. This is how you can know *before* you do something if it will likely improve or erode your financial future.

I assure you that the task before you is not difficult and the resulting financial options and advantages that will open up for you are well worth it. Your increased financial success will not only provide more support for yourself and family but also for people and causes that are important and dear to you.

Bibliography

1. U.S. Census Bureau, 2000 population survey; http://www.census.gov/prod/2002pubs/p23-210.pdf

2. Franklin, Benjamin, "Poor Richard's Almanack", 1732-1758

3. Edmunds.com, Cost-to-Own applet, June 2012

4. U.S. Census Bureau, 2000 population survey; http://www.census.gov/prod/2002pubs/p23-210.pdf

5. U.S. Bureau of Labor Statistics, Current Population Survey, 2009

6. Abkemeier, Noel, "Segmenting The Middle Market: Retirement Risks and Solutions," Society of Actuaries, 2009

7. Hutcheson, James, "The End of a 1,400-Year-Old Business," *Businessweek*, April 16, 2007

8. Robert Hiltonsmith, "The Retirement Savings Drain: Hidden and Excessive Costs of 401(k)s," Demos Policy Research, May 29, 2012

9. An ounce of gold in 1913 was $20.67 and today in 2012 it is $1,600. Mathematically, the dollar's value has fallen by 100%-(20.67/1600), or 98.8%. These gold prices are courtesy of MeasuringWorth.com

10. Lofton, Lloyd, "Filial Responsibility and Long-Term Care," *National Underwriter Life & Health*, May 22, 2012

11. Buffett, Mary and Clark, David, "The Tao of Warren Buffett," 2006

12. Bengen, William, "Determining Withdrawal Rates Using Historical Data," *Journal of Financial Planning*, October 1994

13. Schiller, Robert, stock market data on the S&P 500 from 1871, http://www.econ.yale.edu/~shiller/data.htm

14. Arnott, Robert; Berkin, Andrew; and Ye, Jia, "The Management and Mismanagement of Taxable Assets," Investment Management Reflections No. 2, 2000

Bibliography

15. Markowitz, Harry, "Portfolio Selection," *Journal of Finance*, March 1952

16. Brinson, Hood, and Beebower, "Determinants of Portfolio Performance," *Financial Analysts Journal*, August 1986

17. The Vanguard 500 Index Fund started by John Bogle in 1976

18. January 1993, introduction of the Standard & Poor's Depositary Receipts in the U.S. with the ETF with the ticker symbol, SPY

19. Dammon, Spatt, and Zhang, "Optimal Asset Location and Allocation with Taxable and Tax-Deferred Investing," *Journal of Finance*, June 2004

20. Gopher, Tsuk, Shalev, and Gophna, "Earliest Gold Artifacts in the Levant," *Current Anthropology*, August 1990

21. Herodotus, "The History," translated by David Grene, 1987

22. Dehghan, Saeed Kamali, "Iran Currency Crisis," *The Guardian*, October 3, 2012

23. Federal Reserve Bank of New York, Public Information Department, http://www.NewYorkFed.org

24. U.S. Federal Reserve statistical data releases, 2008-2012

25. Dellith, Erik, "Gold Remains a Poor Inflation Hedge," using Reuters data from 1968 to 2006, SeekingAlpha.com, November 2006

26. Data from Bloomberg.com

27. Walsh, Thomas, "How Much Should A Person Save For Retirement?," TIAA-CREF Institute, November 2003

28. Ibbotson, Xiong, Kreitler, Kreitler, and Chen, "National Savings Rate Guidelines for Individuals," Journal of Financial Planning, April 2007

29. Pfau, Wade, "Safe Savings Rates: A New Approach to Retirement Planning over the Life Cycle," *Journal of Financial Planning*, May 2011

Glossary

Accrue To increase by addition.

Amortization Gradually paying off a debt in regular installments.

Assayed An expert test to determine the composition of an object.

Asset An item with exchangeable value to others.

Asset Class A group of investments with unique risk and return characteristics; such as stocks, bonds, real estate, commodities.

Asset Protection Legal strategies to protect what you own from creditor lawsuits.

Capital Gain The difference between the purchase price and sale price of an investment.

Compounding The process of interest or dividends earning additional interest or dividends on itself by reinvestment.

Disposition The settlement or sale of an item.

Dividends The portion of a company's profit that is paid to shareholders.

Due Diligence A formal investigation process on an investment to determine everything that is true or false about it.

Duration A measure of bond price volatility to interest rates.

Endowment A non-profit institution's donated investment fund.

Entity A legal structure with its own separate existence.

ETF An acronym for exchange-traded fund, a fund that trades like a stock on an exchange.

Fiduciary A person with an obligation to act in someone else's best financial interest.

Maturity The date when an obligation or debt is due.

Insolvent Being unable to pay your creditors, or your debts exceed your assets.

Pension An employer's fund that is invested for the withdrawal of employees during retirement.

Tax-Deferred When income is received now but taxes on that are not due until later.

Unrealized A profit or loss that has not yet been closed and actualized.

Index

Index

About the Author

Duke Kunkler has two degrees in finance and works in venture capital and international business development. His professional background includes trading, accounting, manufacturing operations, advertising research, investment analysis, and acquisition consulting. He advises on how to think about money, careers, and investing. Duke's work or contributions have appeared in *Car and Driver, Boost, Popular Mechanics,* and *Trader Monthly.*

The author can be reached at *FinancialLiteracyBook.com.*

CPSIA information can be obtained
at www.ICGtesting.com
Printed in the USA
FSOW03n2116280816
24324FS